ROBERT LENKIEWICZ
SELF-PORTRAITS

ACKNOWLEDGMENTS

The publishers would like to thank the following individuals for their assistance during the preparation of this publication and the exhibition *Robert Lenkiewicz: Self-Portraits 1956–2002* at the Ben Uri Gallery, The London Jewish Museum of Art, 26 September–16 November 2008.

Fiona Alper	John Lenkiewicz
Jeny Bremer	Mouse Mills
Graham Carey	Freya Mitton of Sotheby's
Lawrie Cleary	Paul Rogers
Louise Courtnell	Anna Navas
Esther Dallaway	Diane Nevitt
Edmund Davari	Stella Ney-Hoch
Helga Edwards of The Halcyon Gallery	Brian and Jane Pollard
Roger Ferris	Matthew Porter
Mark Fielding	Eddie Powell
Nick Fox	Monica Quirk
Daniel Goddard of Bearne's	Lars Ramskold
Dave Goodwin	Chris Robinson
Paul Green of The Halcyon Gallery	Nahem Shoa
Trevor Grimsdale	Paul Somerville of The Somerville Gallery
Nick Grodhunce	Julian Wan
Derek Harris	Ross Winmill

ROBERT LENKIEWICZ
SELF-PORTRAITS

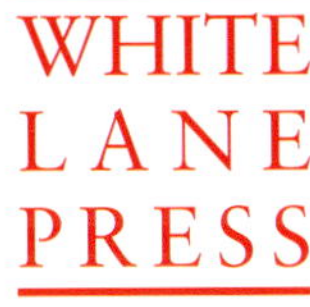

WHITE
LANE
PRESS

Published by White Lane Press 2008
10 9 8 7 6 5 4 3 2 1

ISBN 13: 978-0-9552667-3-7

White Lane Press
38 New Street
Plymouth
Devon PL1 2NA
t: 01752 221450

www.whitelanepress.co.uk

This catalogue is published to coincide with the exhibition
Robert Lenkiewicz: Self-Portraits 1956–2002 at the
Ben Uri Gallery, The London Jewish Museum of Art
26 September–16 November 2008

Edited by M. A. Penwill and Francis Mallett

Printed and bound in Italy by Printer Trento

CONTENTS

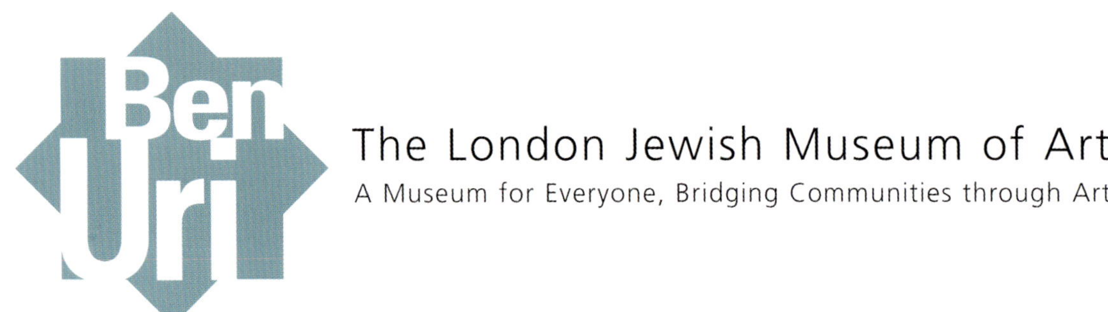

SHORT HISTORY AND MISSION STATEMENT

Ben Uri Gallery is Britain's oldest Jewish cultural organisation. It was founded by Lazar Berson in 1915 in London's East End as an art society to provide support for Jewish artists and craftspeople who were working in the face of poverty, anti-semitism and isolation from the mainstream. It was named after Bezalel Ben Uri, the craftsman who designed and built the Ark of the Covenant in biblical times.

It is Europe's only dedicated Jewish Museum of Art, working in partnership with secular and Jewish museums in the UK and internationally.

The gallery and museum is an educational institution dedicated to enhancing the quality of life of all those upon whom it impacts. It embraces a new broad and fully inclusive role for museums in today's society and addresses contemporary issues through art and its social history.

By fostering easy access, greater appreciation and both social and academic enjoyment of the visual arts, there is an ongoing opportunity to demonstrate its value as a robust and unique bridge between the cultural, religious and political differences and beliefs of our fellow citizens.

Its purpose is to enable the largest possible audience, drawn from the widest possible communities from both home and abroad, to explore for inspiration, learning and enjoyment, the work, lives and contribution of British and European artists of Jewish descent, placed where relevant alongside their non-Jewish contemporaries within the artistic and social context of the national cultural heritage. Through this wide and open outreach 'A Museum for Everyone, Bridging Communities through Art' is achieved.

Its principal route to achieving this is by enabling broad, easy and straightforward physical and visual access – through location, publication, Internet and outreach – to the following:

- The Permanent Collection: the largest of its kind in the world, accessed physically or virtually via continued exhibition, research, conservation and acquisition.

- Temporary Exhibitions: curating, touring and hosting important internationally focused exhibitions of the widest artistic appeal that, without the museum's focus, would not be seen in the UK. Kids always free!

- Publications: commissioning new academic research on the artists and their historical context to accompany the museum's exhibitions.

- Library and Archive: a resource dating from the turn of the 20th century, documenting and tracing in parallel the artistic and social development of the Ben Uri and Jewish artists working or exhibiting in Britain as part of the evolving British historical landscape.

- Education Programmes: for adults, students, schoolchildren and artists, through symposia, lectures, student teaching packs, visits, after school art clubs and free family art days.

- Artists: monthly artist peer group programmes, Ben Uri International Jewish Artists of the Year Awards competition, guidance and affiliation benefits.

- Care in the Community: through the pioneering pilot project between the Ben Uri and the British Association of Art Therapists.

- Website: providing an online educational and access tool, to function as a virtual gallery and artists' reference resource for students, collectors and scholars.

To continue our objectives and fulfil the museum's potential Ben Uri desperately needs to relocate to the heart of central London and is currently seeking *c.*2000 sq. m to establish a permanent museum and exhibition space that will be both an international centre of scholarship and an exciting hub of activity for our local communities.

CHAIRMAN'S INTRODUCTION

Ben Uri Gallery, The London Jewish Museum of Art initiates exhibitions which explore the lives and work of artists of European Jewish descent within an art rather than a religious context. This catalogue, which accompanies an important and revealing exhibition, of *Self-Portraits: 1956–2002*, provides a powerful and convincing platform for a critical reassessment of Robert Lenkiewicz's place amongst his peers.

Lenkiewicz was born in 1941 from refugee stock. His father, a horse breeder from Poland, and his mother, a German baroness, escaped the Nazi persecution in Germany in 1939, just in time to avoid the horrors of the Holocaust. They married in London in 1940, settling in Cricklewood, and opened the Hotel Shemtov in Fordwych Road, primarily a home for Jewish émigrés.

This environment provided a diverse and immediately accessible variety of subject matter during Lenkiewicz's formative years. He was an instinctive and prodigious talent, drawing at every opportunity. He was admitted to Central St Martin's at the age of only sixteen on the strength of a series of anatomical drawings of dissected pigeons. From there, he moved on to the Royal Academy Schools but he found the conformity too inhibiting and was expelled for non-attendance. Already his very individual future direction was being mapped out, as he worked in a deeply unfashionable figurative style, often on an equally unfashionable large scale, with his subject matter being the disadvantaged of society, including alcoholics, addicts and down-and-outs.

Nothing about Lenkiewicz falls into any traditional or expected category. He demonstrated a disregard, if not contempt, for the commercial requirements of his practice. His deep engagement with the tradition of philosophical thought encouraged his ambition to articulate his views about society on canvas, as a journalist would in newsprint. Uniquely amongst post-war British artists, Lenkiewicz conceived of his paintings not as individual works but as related parts of 'Projects': large scale exhibitions of paintings on specific themes related to 'the business of living'. Themes such as *Vagrancy* (1973), *Mental Handicap* (1976), *Old Age* (1979) and *Death* (1982) examined in depth the effects of human isolation and brought wide public attention to sections of the community generally considered taboo.

In a complementary series of inquiries, Lenkiewicz also investigated the nature of personal relationships in ironically titled Projects such as *Love & Romance* (1975) and *Love & Mediocrity* (1976), and then human physiology in a state of crisis in *Jealousy* (1977), *Orgasm* (1978) and *The Painter with Mary: A Study in Obsessional Behaviour* (1981). His conclusion, that intense feeling isolates people rather than bringing them together, led to a remarkable physiological theory of human nature: that intense aesthetic attraction, whether towards other people or equally towards ideas or beliefs, took us down 'the straight road to fascism'. Thus his Projects, and his 20,000 volume private library, were intended as 'an investigation of the origins of fascism by enquiring into obsessional behaviour in all its forms'.

For this exhibition, curated by Francis Mallett, Ben Uri has chosen to focus on a survey of his revealing and challenging self-portraits as the subject of his first London museum show. It was a theme that Lenkiewicz examined in detail through the 1978 Project on *Self-Portrait*, an ironic look at the notion that the self-portrait (or any portrait, for that matter) is somehow revelatory of the 'essence' of the sitter. 'I wondered what it would be like just to paint myself; to paint what I saw in the mirror repetitively. Well, within half a sitting I became aware that all I was doing was painting a picture of a mirror; there just happened to be something there reflected in the mirror.'

The collected self-portraits here represent a distributed 'project' that allows us to witness Lenkiewicz recording the passing of time in his own life; from the open gaze of a fifteen-year-old in Cricklewood to the harrowing image painted shortly before his premature death, aged only sixty, in Plymouth in 2002.

This exhibition and catalogue, a book by any other name, attempts to give the visitor and reader a glimpse into the complex life of Robert Lenkiewicz and an insight into the development of the mind of a unique thinker and highly individual painter. On your and the museum's behalf, I thank all the lenders for their spontaneous support, the exhibition and catalogue sponsors, both corporate and private, without whom this exhibition would not have fulfilled its potential, and naturally my colleagues at the museum, led by Suzanne Lewis, for their commitment and expertise.

I am very proud that Ben Uri Gallery, The London Jewish Museum of Art, is the first London museum to provide this survey of an artist who has been too often sensationalised rather than critically assessed within his peer group of post-war British and European artists.

David J. Glasser

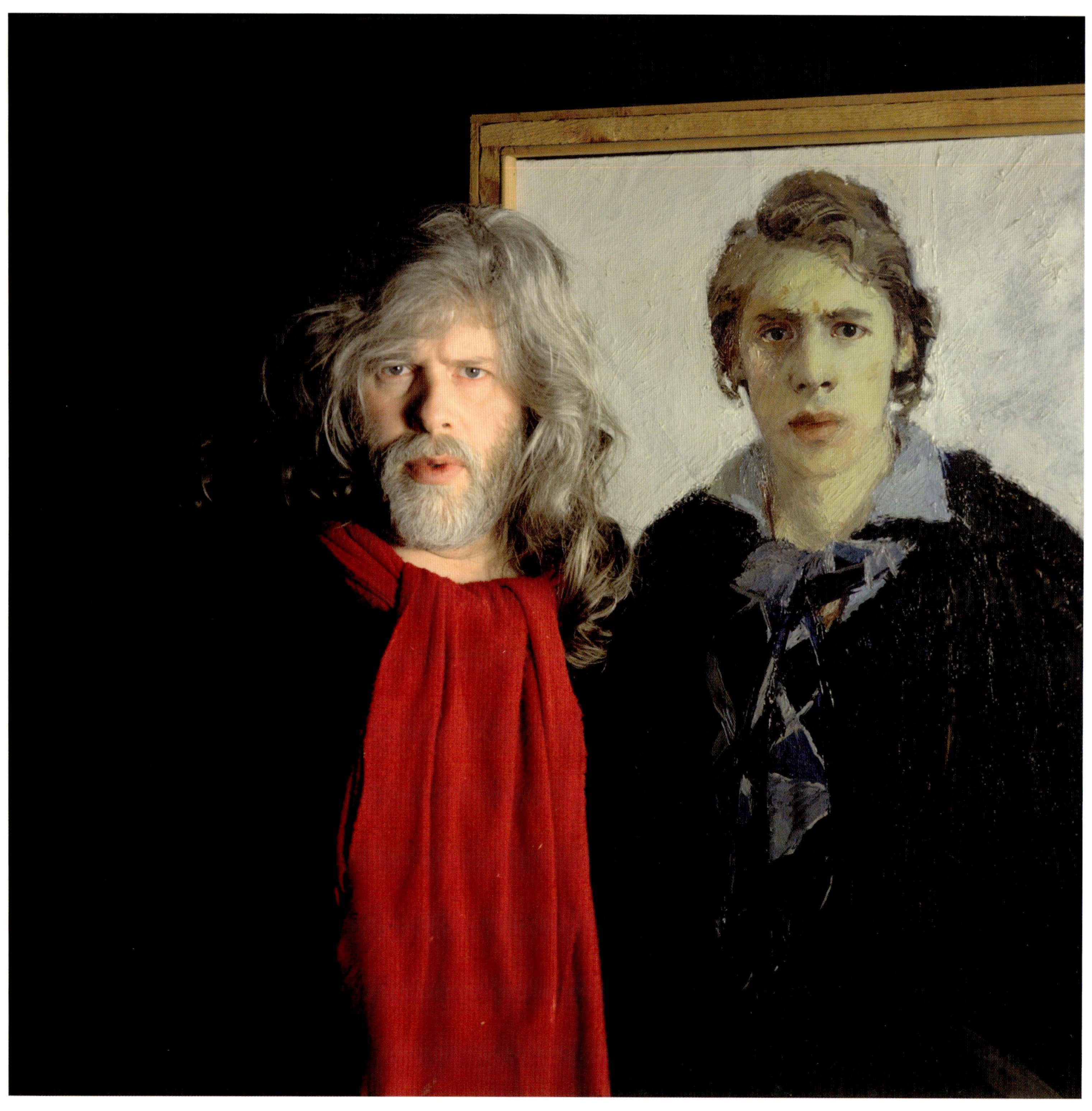

Robert Lenkiewicz in 1993 with the canvas *Self-Portrait With Punch Magazine*, painted when the artist was sixteen years old.

INTRODUCTION

Tom L. Freudenheim

Obsessive! That describes Robert Lenkiewicz – at least insofar as we can know him through his art. But isn't that a description of many, perhaps most, artists? Yet the obsessions of Lenkiewicz are so varied – starting out with his haunting vanity – that it's instructive to note where his paintings succeed, why so many of them don't, and why the painter himself remains so mysterious, despite a fairly transparent biography. After all, he articulated his own thoughts about society, painting, self-portraiture, his deep feelings for the art of the past, and his sense of continuity with that tradition.

His forays into abstraction or landscape or still-life have the feel of student work, even when executed in mid life. What a contrast with his portraiture! We can understand Lenkiewicz as willing to try a range of expressions, but we also note his triumphal successes as a painter of people, using a range of models but ultimately starring himself. He knew he was 'playing at Rembrandt' by constantly taking yet another look at himself. So, like the great Dutch master, Lenkiewicz grows old before our eyes – in fact and (unlike Rembrandt) in fantasy: he paints himself as an old man and even on his deathbed while still young. A final irony of the recurrent *thanatos* we see in his paintings was the artist's death at age sixty.

What are we to make of such vanity? The simplest answer is to dismiss it as the megalomania of a second-rate painter with higher aspirations. But that's grossly unfair, since the immense *oeuvre* may be strangely uneven, but its high points are numerous, with an astonishing number of compelling paintings. In fact, Lenkiewicz is a painter of extraordinary skill and power, and if his occasionally unsuccessful experimentation led in directions that didn't pan out, this does nothing to diminish the sense of wonder that we find in so much of the best work – especially in his uncanny ability to portray himself and others with whose facial or bodily attitudes he could play manipulative games. And play he did, sometimes in ways that suggested frivolity but more often through suggestive and enigmatic ways in which the viewer cannot necessarily discern a clear point of view. Surely that uncertainty is very intentional, as Lenkiewicz very evidently doesn't want to let us in on the full meaning of so many of the paintings. Or perhaps it's as simple as understanding that the immense body of work he produced reflects a very clear point of view: the need to paint!

Portraits of vagrants – especially photo essays – have become almost fashionable in the past several decades, with increasing public discussion about homelessness. The viewer ends up participating in a kind of unsavoury voyeurism that suggests social action but actually is nothing more than passive ogling. Lenkiewicz never moves in that direction because his engagement with his subjects – even when they are street people – is so intensely personal. He could be one of them; occasionally his self-portraits even suggest that perhaps he is. Or *we* could be one of them. He cares as much for Syd sniffing glue as for the old women in the alms house; and as much for those subjects as for his favourite: himself. The work suggests a joy in painting: a subject is seen as colourful or 'paint-worthy' and then receives the kind of loving attention that almost never conveys social judgments. This is a painter who doesn't care about evoking empathy; rather, he wants to engage us in the magical powers of painting, *his* painting. So we admire the work more for what it says about the power of art as art than about what one or another of the depictions might suggest about the people on view.

That's true despite the presumably meaningful allusions Lenkiewicz makes to art of the past. He is obviously well acquainted with Italian Renaissance painting, but is especially enamoured of the seventeenth century Spanish masters – Velázquez, Ribera – with suggestions of the French, especially the brothers Le Nain and Manet; and the spectre of Rembrandt hovers over it all. For an artist, whose parents were Jewish refugees from Nazi Germany and ran a London hostel for other displaced refugees, it's worth considering how that personal history doesn't appear to enter directly into his work. Instead, Lenkiewicz often removes himself psychologically from the specific historical moment and enters that larger world of 'art' in which there are few chronological boundaries because the subjects – often Biblical – really exist out of time. This distance from a particular moment in time (e.g. would we be able to date his paintings if we were simply to come upon them somewhere?) also permits – or perhaps pushes – Lenkiewicz in the direction of Christological subject matter. For him it's not just the association with the wider world of art, but also the exit from anything that might be seen as Jewish. Doesn't he revel in the Christ-like image that he makes for himself? And isn't it also rebellious to place that same image into sexually suggestive contexts, such as orgasm and bestiality? If the artist is not a revolutionary in terms of technique or formal concerns, then he will find other means of expressing personal rebellion.

Removal from London was surely one of these ways. But was that really removal? Lenkiewicz engaged in so many kinds of megalomanical endeavours – from the apparently endless range of expansive art projects to the hoax of placing an obituary for himself – that one wonders whether distance from London really worked, other than providing more affordable space for a studio and massive library accretions. There's a special irony in a figurative artist's self-exile from London during the flowering of the so-called School of London. Those mostly Jewish artists were emphatically more avant-garde in their attempts at reconceiving figurative art, and only Kitaj ventured into the realm of Jewish references. In one way or another all of them were willing to confront the challenges that abstraction had set ever since Cézanne. With his vast collection of art books and sophisticated understanding of art history, Lenkiewicz was aware of those challenges, and even took them up with limited success. But his real strength was in creating paintings that suggest there never was a Cézanne or Picasso; better to ignore than to confront.

Nowhere is that more evident than in the amazing array of self-portraits. Revealing himself in many guises – with women, in sexual poses, as a pot-bellied naked middle-aged man, as participant in mythology and history and religion – it's unclear whether Lenkiewicz ever actually reveals himself at all. Unlike the Lucas Samaras Polaroid photos that show the artist in a variety of homoerotic and self-mutilating poses, these Lenkiewicz self-portraits are more about an artist looking at a variety of ways in which he can study himself as a fit subject for painting. It's interesting to speculate on how much of that is a homage to Picasso, whose erotic self-portraiture he surely knew.

We take note of the artist ageing but, even more significantly, we take note of the artist as an extraordinarily adept painter. Because he uses himself in so many guises, it's difficult to get as engaged with the person in the art as we are with the art itself. And looking at Lenkiewicz coupling with a goat never looks like a crude publicity stunt, as does Jeff Koons having sex with his celebrity porn star wife, Ilona Staller. (Had Koons ever seen Lenkiewicz's work, which predates his own sexual self-display?)

The best of this work deserves more serious attention, not only because there is so much exciting and satisfying painting, although that would suffice. Knowing how to play with detail – emphasise some details while intentionally fudging others – enables us to enter these paintings with the illusion that we enter their subjects as well. But art is *about* illusion, and repeated study of the Lenkiewicz *oeuvre* makes manifest that we only imagine that we know what we're looking at. The artist has cleverly drawn us into the magic of his technique and choice of subject, while making certain that we are kept at bay from a full understanding of what was in his mind. That's appropriate to a man with a wide-ranging intellect and a voracious appetite for knowledge of the world around him as well as the esoteric unseen world of his amazing imagination.

Tom L. Freudenheim
New York, 2008

Tom L. Freudenheim is an art historian and former Director of The Baltimore Museum of Art and Assistant Secretary for Museums at the Smithsonian Institution. He is now retired and lives in New York City.

The Self-Portraits

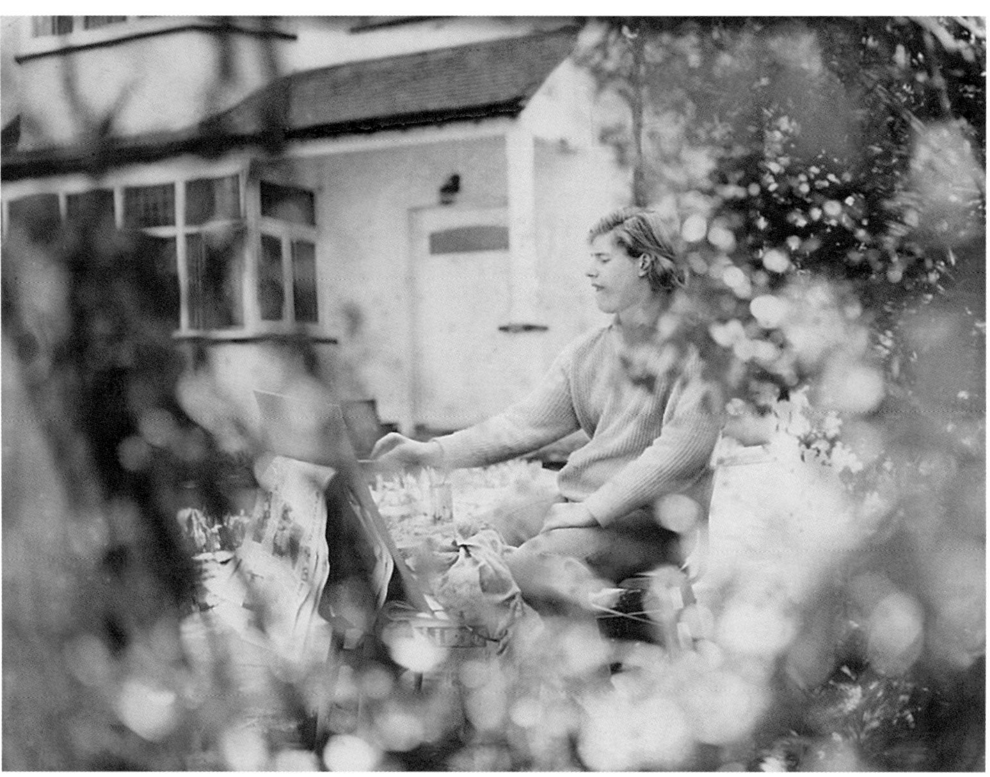

Robert Lenkiewicz aged fifteen years painting in the garden of the Hotel Shemtov. *Photo*: S. Ney-Hoch.

*c.*1955
Self-Portrait in Room No. 3.
Poster paint on paper laid on board.
56 x 38 cm.

*c.*1956
Self-Portrait Aged 16.
Oil on board.
23 x 15 cm.

Robert Lenkiewicz (RL): It was a kind of Jewish kosher hotel, and there were various sorts of scholarly types; it was a combination of rabbis and lunatics. People having been dropped by their parents because they were no longer in control, people who'd been dropped by their sons and daughters because they weren't in control. Mother was a sort of nursemaid to about thirty people who paid her a nominal weekly rent for board and lodging.

I worked prolifically and totally obsessively in Room 3, with the green lino. When I look back on it now, I was as crazed as the rest of them.

I remember even having an exhibition in my room that my brother Johnny helped with, and we charged a penny entrance fee. I remember Mrs Kempner, stone deaf, coming in. It was such a strange thing for them to see; all these portraits – they would never have been painted in their lives. They were all from Russia, Lithuania and Poland, a completely different kind of thing. 'Thou shalt make no graven image' was absolutely inherent in their culture.

R.O. Lenkiewicz
In conversation with F. Mallett and M. A. Penwill, June 1997

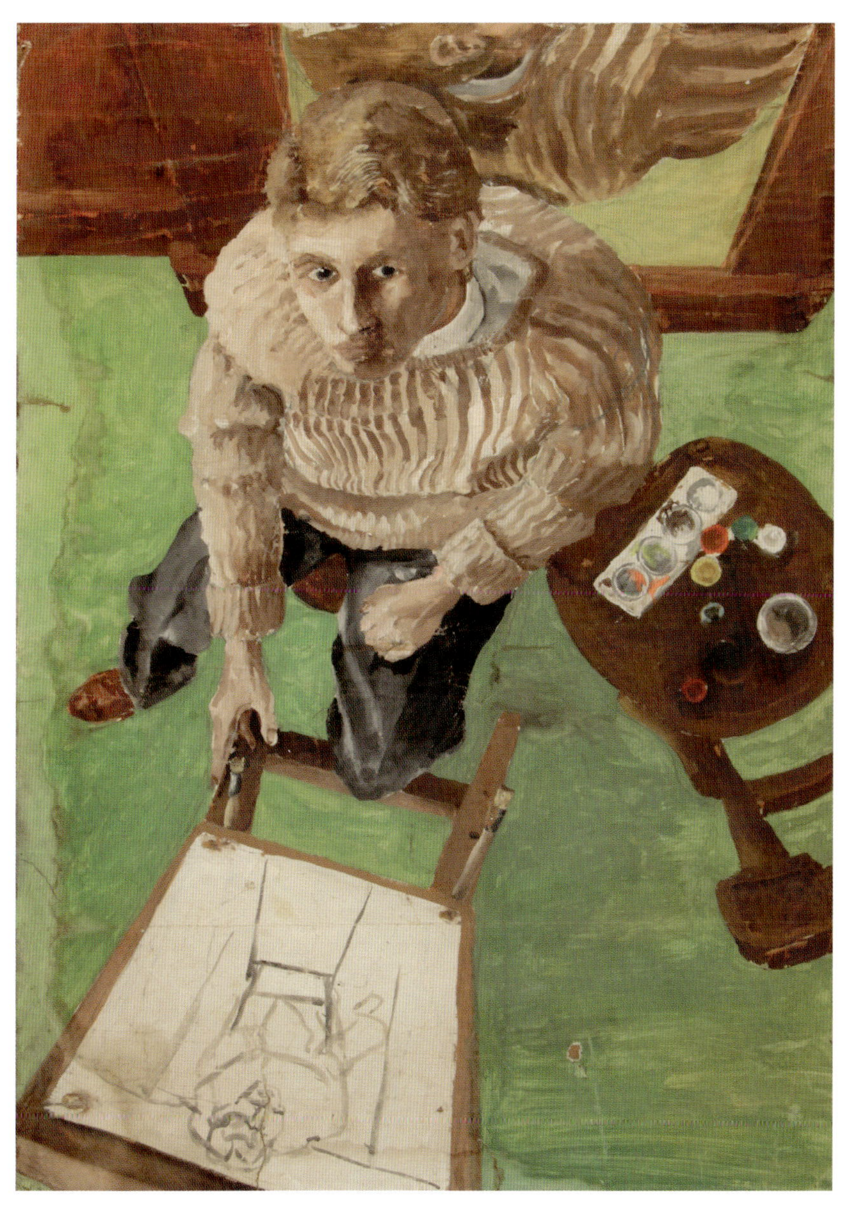

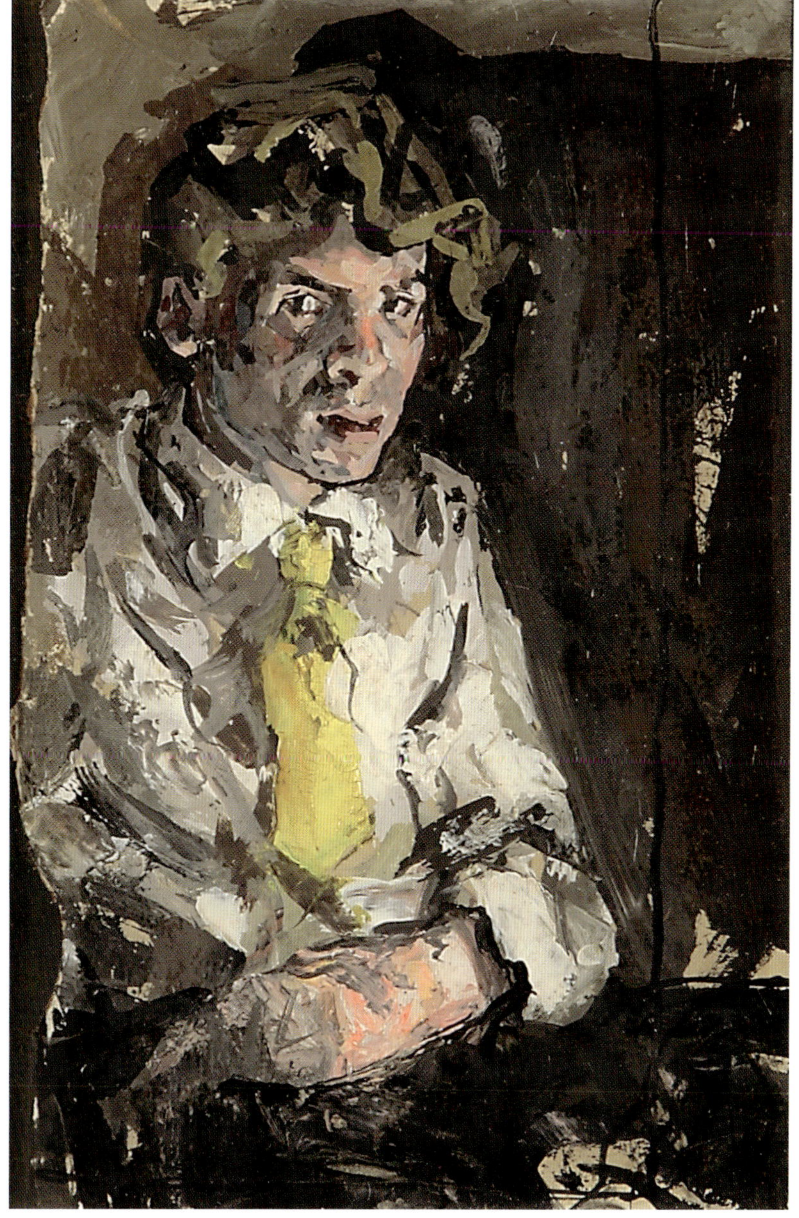

*c.*1956
Self-Portrait.
Pencil on paper.
21 x 16 cm.

*c.*1956
Self-Portrait.
Oil on board.
21 x 16 cm.

1956
Self-Portrait Aged 15.
Oil on board.
27 x 17 cm.

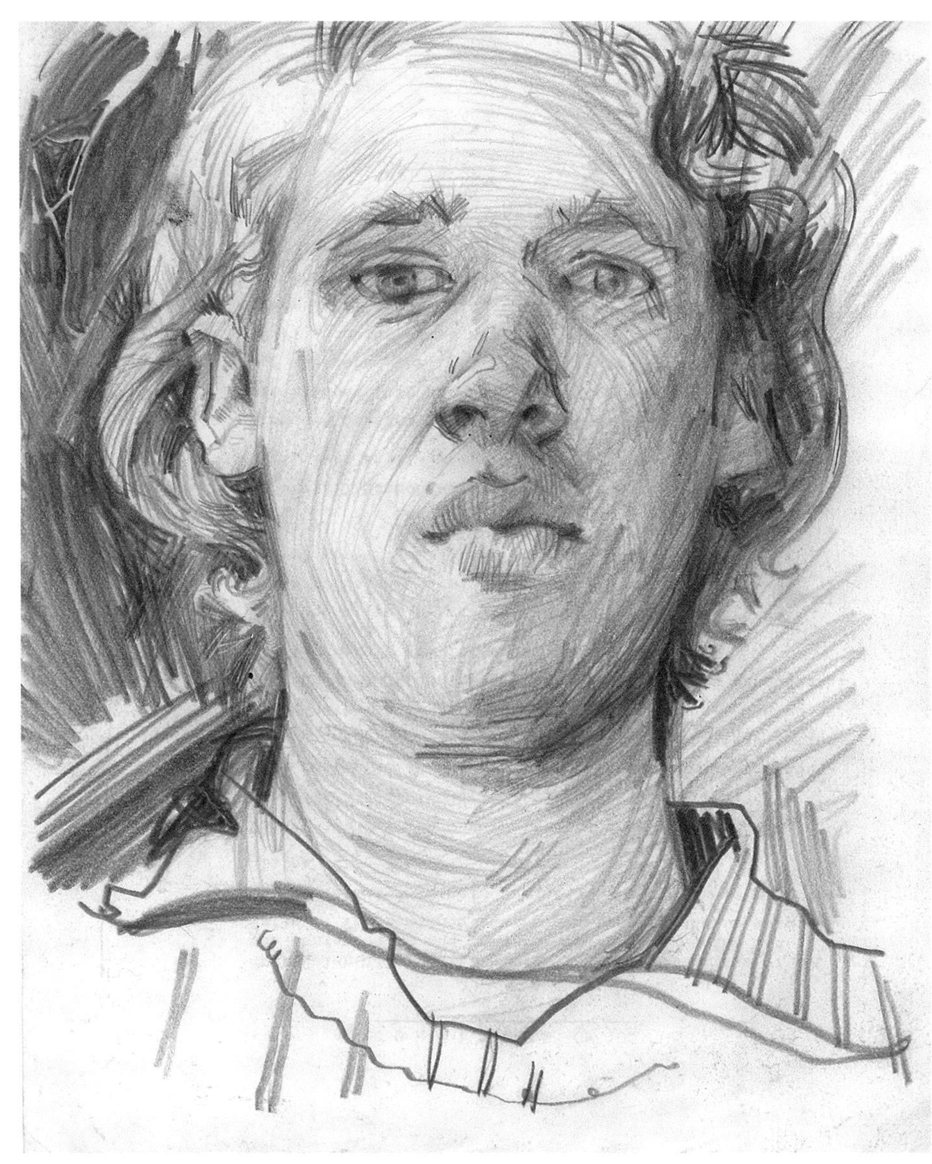

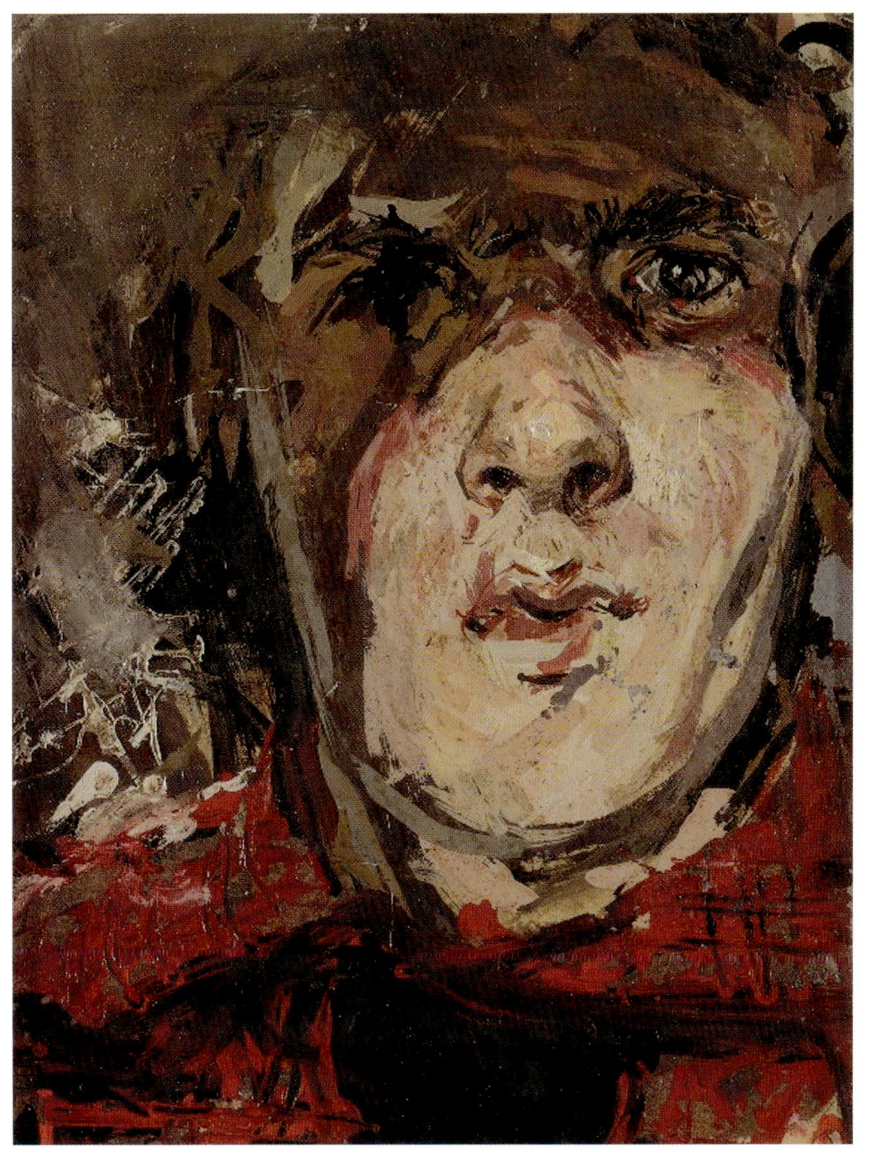
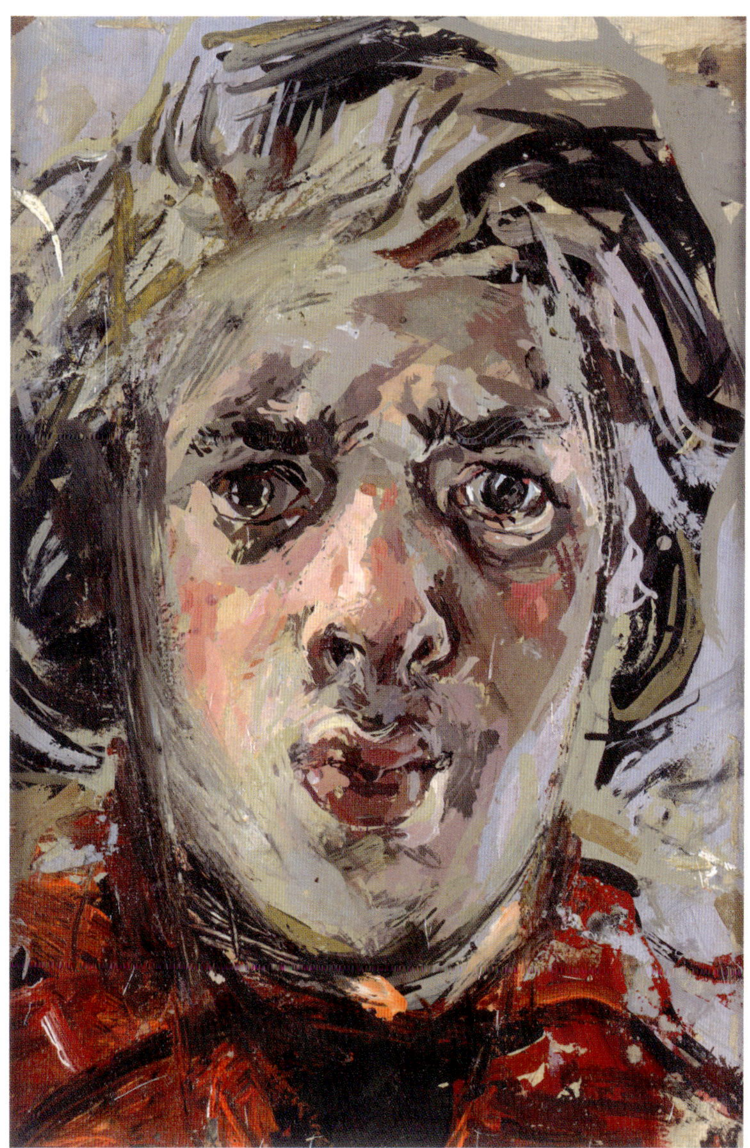

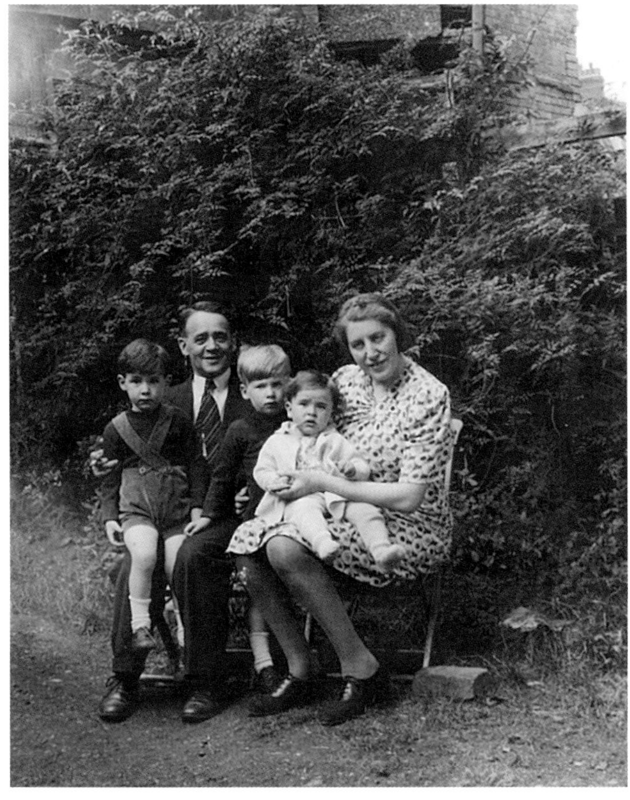

The Lenkiewicz family in 1946. Left to right: Bernard, Isaac, Robert, John and Alice. *Photo*: courtesy of S. Ney-Hoch.

*c.*1956
Self-Portrait.
Oil on paper.
29 x 18 cm.

RL: [Ma] encouraged my painting tremendously.

My mother's father was, she claimed, the court painter to Ludwig of Bavaria. My brother went to Munich to find this alleged gravestone that was supposed to be a very handsome thing adjacent to the medical practitioner who had discovered the cure for syphilis – ironic in particular as according to my mother, certainly in conversations with me, that's what my grandfather died of, though I think my brothers know nothing of that or certainly think that's fanciful. He was Bernard von Schloss-Berg, court painter to the King and painted those decorative Wagnerian fantasies on the ceilings of the castles.

My brother did find a gravestone; it was not magisterial and baroquely carved; it was a small, little stone, a slate, tipped upside down, the name embedded in the earth. He corrected its position and indeed it did say Baron von Schloss-Berg indicating that he was certainly knighted for *something*.

RL: I suppose the turning point in my relationship with her was when I was about thirteen. I'd painted her and thought, 'My goodness, this is rather good!' I took the painting upstairs and put it on my easel by the bed. I thought I would go downstairs and get a hot water bottle and some cocoa for bed, not look at the painting and then sit myself up comfortably in bed and finally look at the portrait and see what I thought of it. An hour later, would I think it was as good as I first thought? I believed it a significant turning point picture.

I did all that; got into bed, puffed up the pillows and prepared to look at it. Then this horrible sinking sensation – the whole portrait had been completely swirled and smudged and scraped in a most violent way. I knew instantly that while I had been down in the kitchen my mother had sneaked up and destroyed the image because she didn't like the way she looked in it! She was a tubby lady and obviously took offence. I tore down the stairs to her room and said, 'Why did you do that?' She said, '*Noh!* It was a terrible picture, a terrible picture.' I said, 'You don't know what you've done. That was a *stupid* thing to do. I can't tell you how angry I am!'

That would have been the turning-point; I tended to freeze off after that.

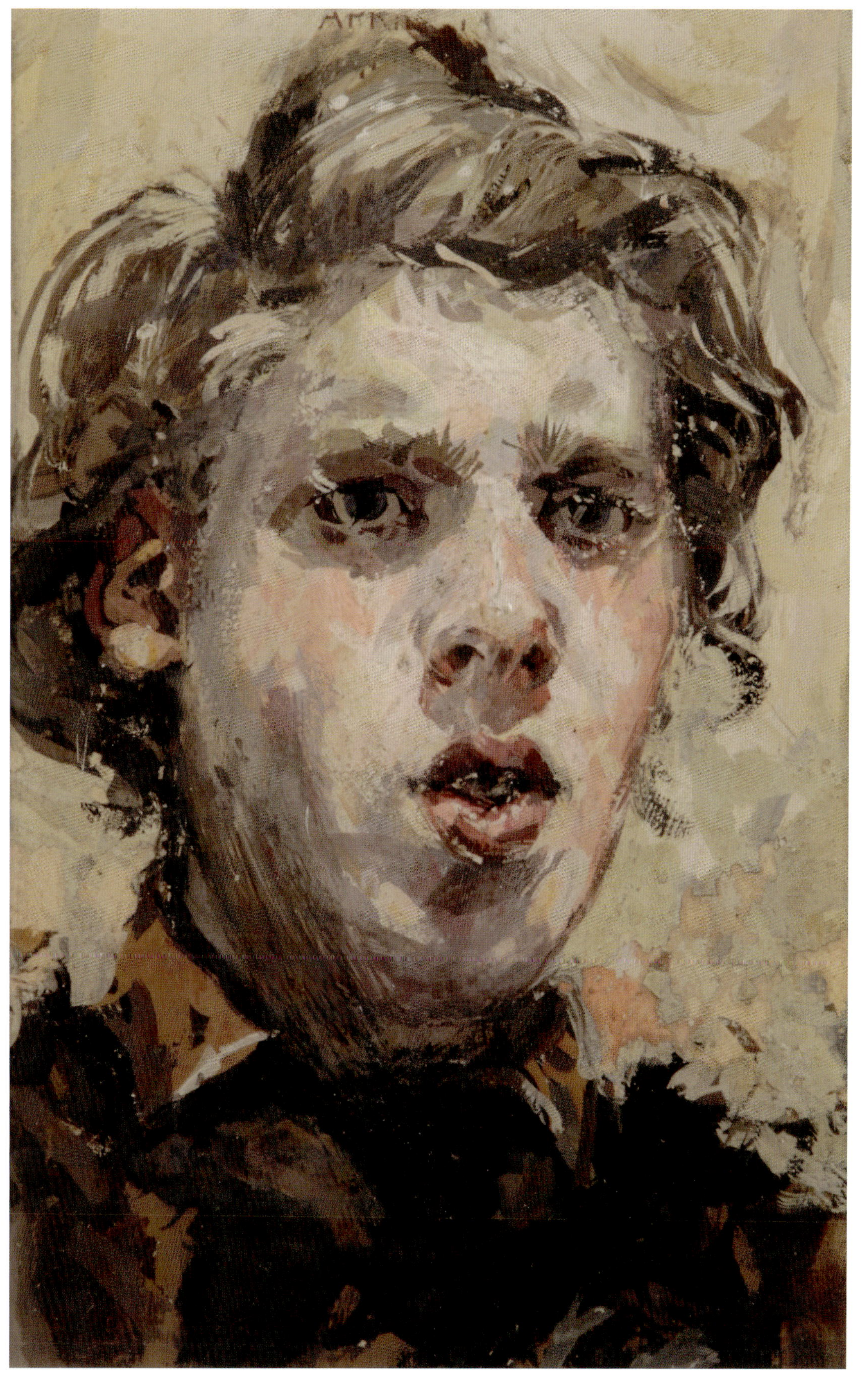

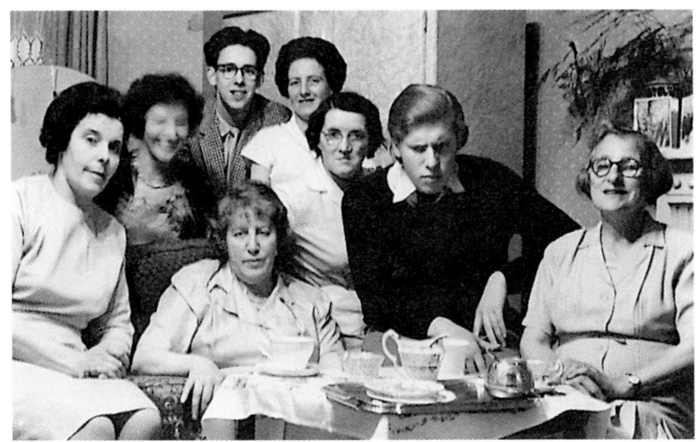

Robert and his non-identical twin Bernard with their mother Alice (seated in armchair) and staff of the Hotel Shemtov, *c.*1957.

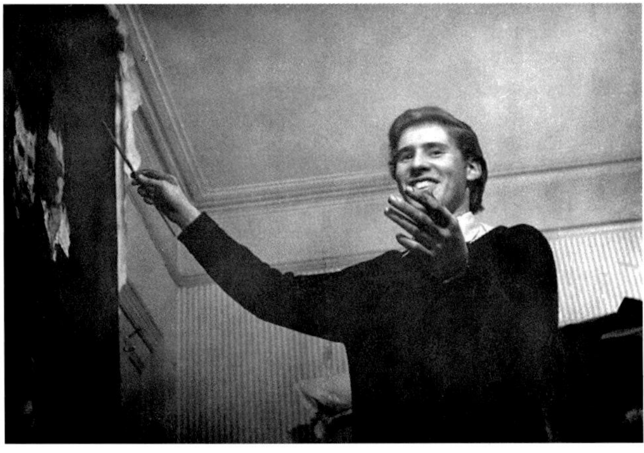

Robert painting in Room 3 of the Hotel Shemtov. *c.*1957.
Photo: S. Ney-Hoch.

*c.*1957
Self-Portrait With Letter.
Oil on canvas.
174 x 100 cm.

RL: [Ma] was very, very upset when I left home. I was getting ready to see Charles Laughton in the film *Rembrandt* on the black and white television. I'd done my duties, I'd served the dinners … and we had some sort of row and she said, 'You would not last five minutes in the real world. What do you know about the real world?' I said, 'I could walk out the front door, turn right or left and I'd get on fine – I just want to work, I'd get on fine.' 'You think so? Then do it, do it!' she shouted.

So I did, then and there.

I didn't come back for nine months. I had nowhere to stay. I walked all the way to Soho. I was at St Martin's, so it must have been when I was sixteen or seventeen. I slept on a doorstep. One thing led to another: I had met an older woman and stayed with her for a while. I remember I left without any desire to inflict distress. I really was determined to be independent. I left quickly; my brothers didn't. I didn't go back, but I know that it upset her deeply. Obviously, as you get older you realise just how much.

Bernard Lenkiewicz [speaking to John Lenkiewicz]: Do you remember when Robert went missing, and I had to locate him, because mum went mad? And I finally found out, I can't remember how, that he was living in either Ellsworthy Road or Fellowes Road in Swiss Cottage. Got in there, and there he was, in bed, with two beautiful girls. Remember that? *I* can remember that! Needless to say, I came back without him.

Westcountry Television film Lenkiewicz: Demon or Delight?
first transmitted 9 May 1996

John Lenkiewicz: She adored Robert, really adored him. My mother was in love with Robert. And I mean *in love*; really i-n l-o-v-e.

In conversation with M. A. Penwill, 2008

RL: I think she was genuinely attached to me. She used to inform me that I was very handsome, a good looking chap. When you're young, you believe this sort of thing – you've got nothing to measure it against; it takes quite a few years to realise that perhaps one person's opinion isn't quite enough. She made a fuss about it, but really I think there was a kind of inverted anti-Semitism there because I was the only blond; my two brothers were swarthy and dark. I don't really know but I think there was a slight 'blond beast' element there. There are other things I could say about that relationship, but it just wouldn't be fair to my brothers.

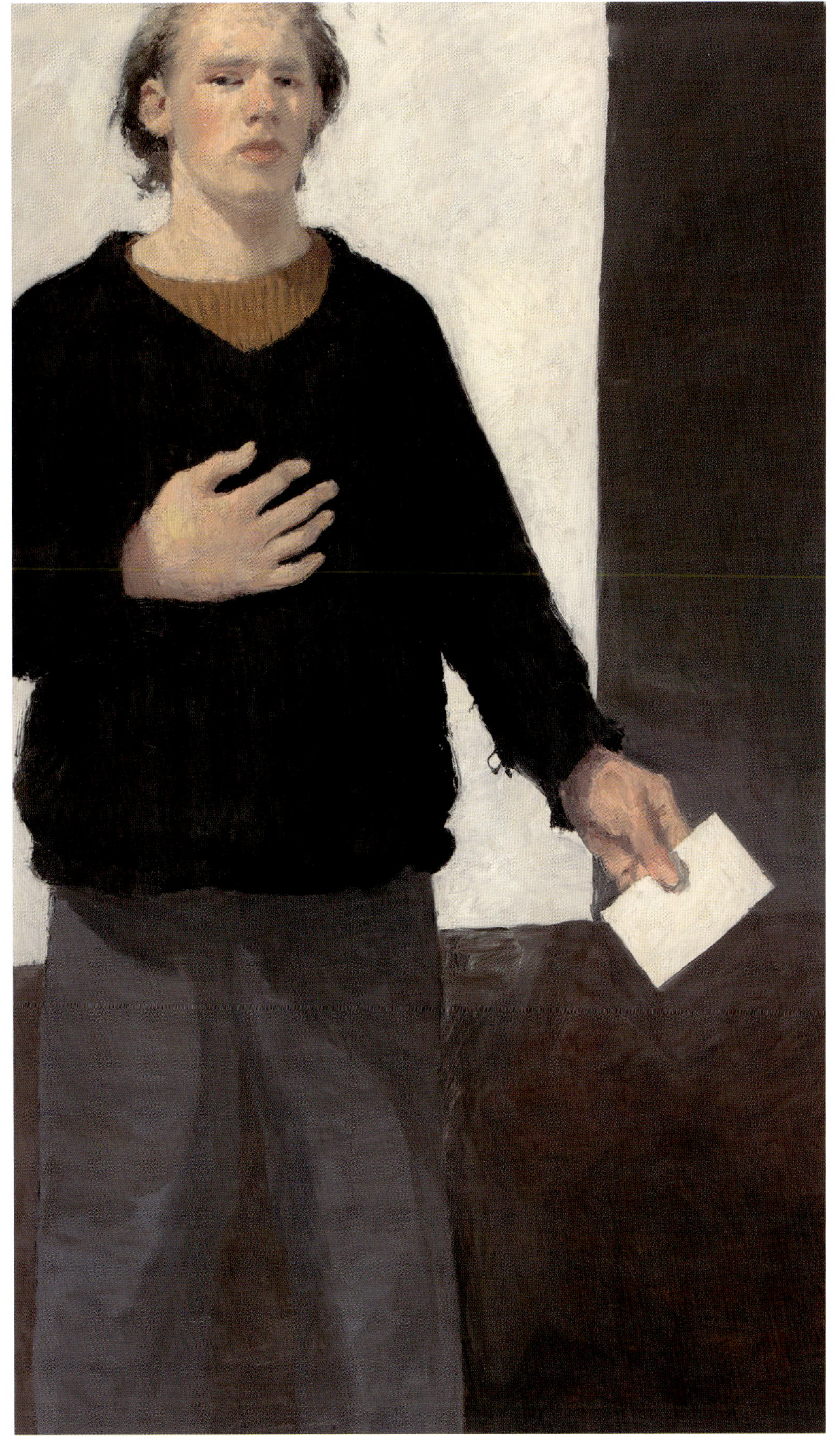

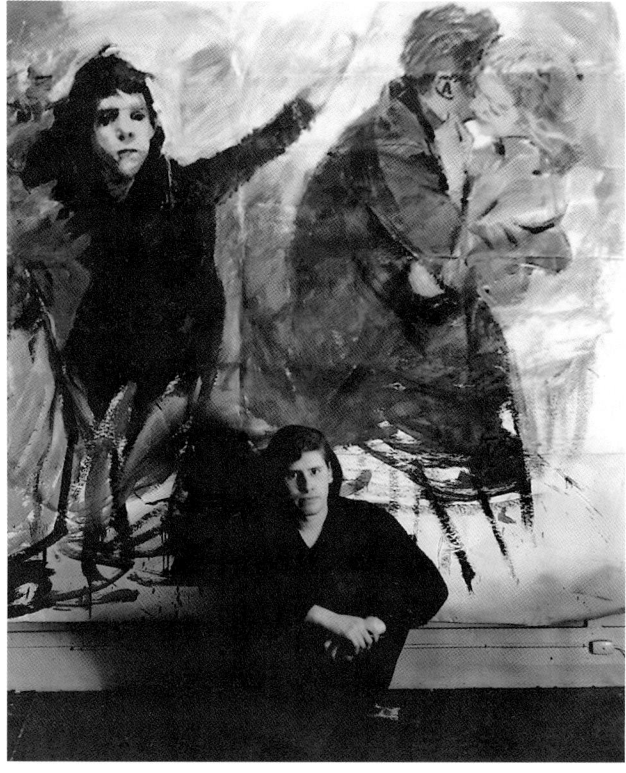

Robert at his Fellowes Road studio, c.1958. The painting is on the theme of 'lovers'. *Photo:* collection of the artist.

1957
Self-Portrait With *Punch* Magazine.
Oil on canvas.
188 x 64 cm.

'I left school and went to St Martin's School of Art in London, and then I got into the Royal Academy, who eventually asked me to leave. I'm still not sure why but it may have had something to do with a crowded canteen one lunchtime – I walked in with a girlfriend sitting on my shoulders, for no particular reason. The place was crowded so I thought we would save space and we ordered our food and went to a table where I sat down to eat with her still on my shoulders, balancing her plate on my head.'

R.O. Lenkiewicz

An Exhibition of Ourselves, *by Jack Holman, Western Morning News, 1993*

'Particularly when I was at the Royal Academy, I was less anxious about worrying about high art. I saw all these young people painting in the style of Rothko, in the style of Barnett Newman, in the style of Hans Hofmann, in the style of Jasper Johns, and I found that discomfiting. What could they possibly know about the thoughts, ideas and feelings of a mathematician from Russia – sixty years old, semi-suicidal, living in New York – at the age of eighteen and painting in that way? To me it seemed dishonourable and weak-charactered, so I just continued sloshing away quite innocently, on a fairly academic basis ...'

Robert Lenkiewicz and Louise Churchill
In conversation on From the Chair, *Plymouth Sound Radio, July 1995*

RL: I lived in the Hampstead area. I would often see people like the kinetic sculptor Kenneth Martin walking up and down the road and one felt very aware of the otherness of what was happening. One didn't give it names like 'elitist' or anything like that but you had the same feeling towards it as you might have to somebody who was preoccupied with mathematics or physics. You looked at it from a distance and wondered what was going on ...

Rothko, Barnett Newman and, funnily enough, Sam Francis – he was the first one where I began to feel that I was responding first of all to the energy and the scale and then this notion of colourfield, of being swamped by something rather than your mental eye enveloping it ... The names of the painters were the same names as the people at my mother's hotel. The Hofmanns and the Rothkoviches and so on ... There was something going on here – these were the Real McCoy, these were Jewish scholars, these were refugee mathematicians. There's *something* going on here, what is it?

I was very interested in relating ethics to aesthetics, even at that time.
I remember using this phrase all the time: 'The only difference is the difference; the only difference is the difference' to avoid value judgements. But that difference was *aesthetic.*

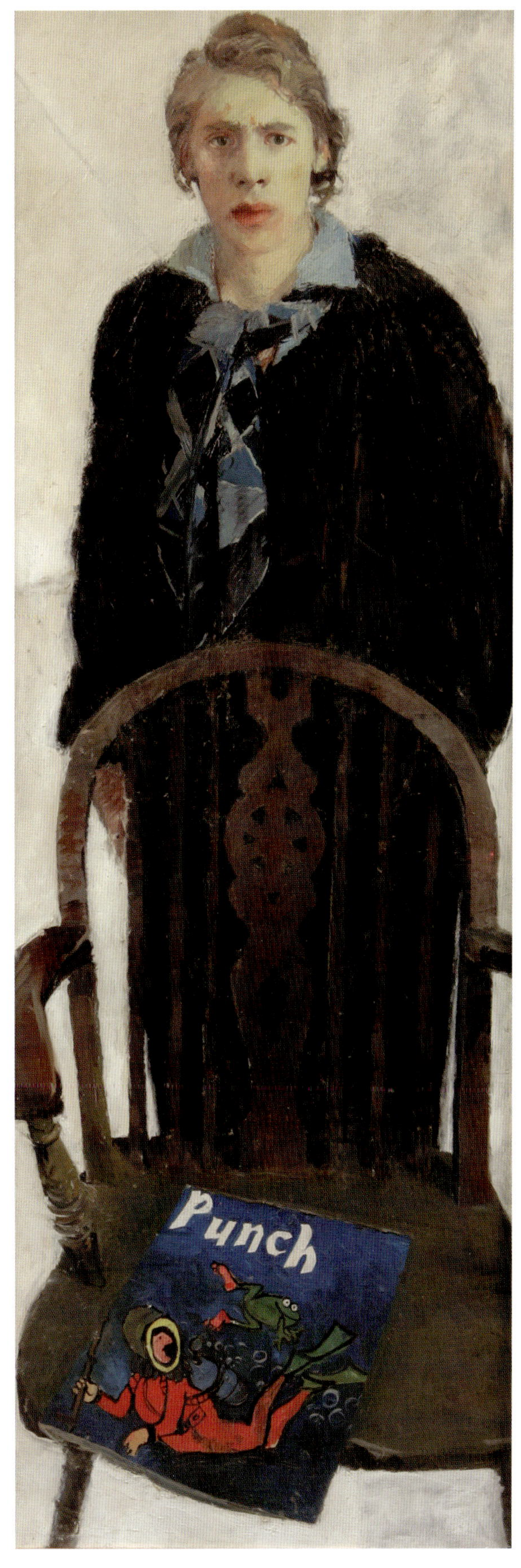
Punch

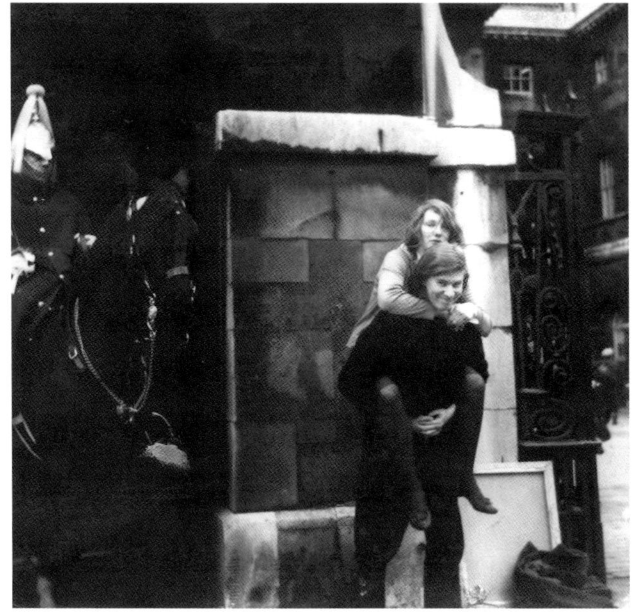

Robert with Celia Mills (Mouse) in 1961. *Photo:* courtesy of C. Mills.

Mouse: I was nearly 17; Robert was 19. He was working in the canteen and I had had a dream that someone was putting up a sign saying 'Canteen Staff Wanted'. I went there and a woman was doing exactly that. Robert and I worked side by side, and that was it.

He was thought extremely strange and a bit of a poseur – a copy of Nietzsche always visible in his coat pocket – but very interesting. What singled Robert out, the thing which gave him an extra edge, was that he had an intense interest in everything. That's also why he was so successful with women; he was extremely interested in what they thought. How many men are interested in what women think? They just want to get over what *they* know!

He was overpoweringly entertaining. Tremendously gifted as a painter. He knew he was skillful, he knew he was 'slick', and that he was undoubtedly very, very clever, but he also knew he didn't have that extra something which made a great painter. 'Sometimes,' he would say, 'I get *near* it.' He used this word all the time: 'flash' – '*That's flash!*' – about illustration. He used to tear down posters in the tube stations, hundreds of them, because he loved the way an illustrator had done something. He loved Courbet, not because he was especially deep, but because he was theatrical and 'flash'.

Mouse Mills and Monica Quirk
In conversation with M. A. Penwill, 2008

1958
Self-Portrait Aged 17.
Oil on board.
59 x 49 cm.

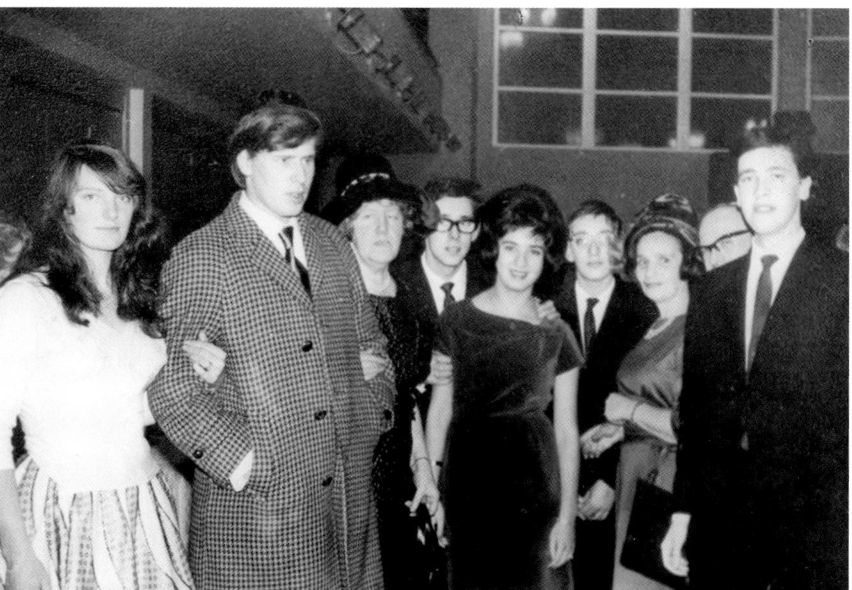

Mouse Mills with Robert at the engagement party of Robert's twin Bernard, 1962. Seen left to right are: Alice Lenkiewicz, Bernard and his fiancée Gillian, her brother Anthony, mother Bella and father Isidore. Robert's brother John is on the right. *Photo:* courtesy of C. Mills.

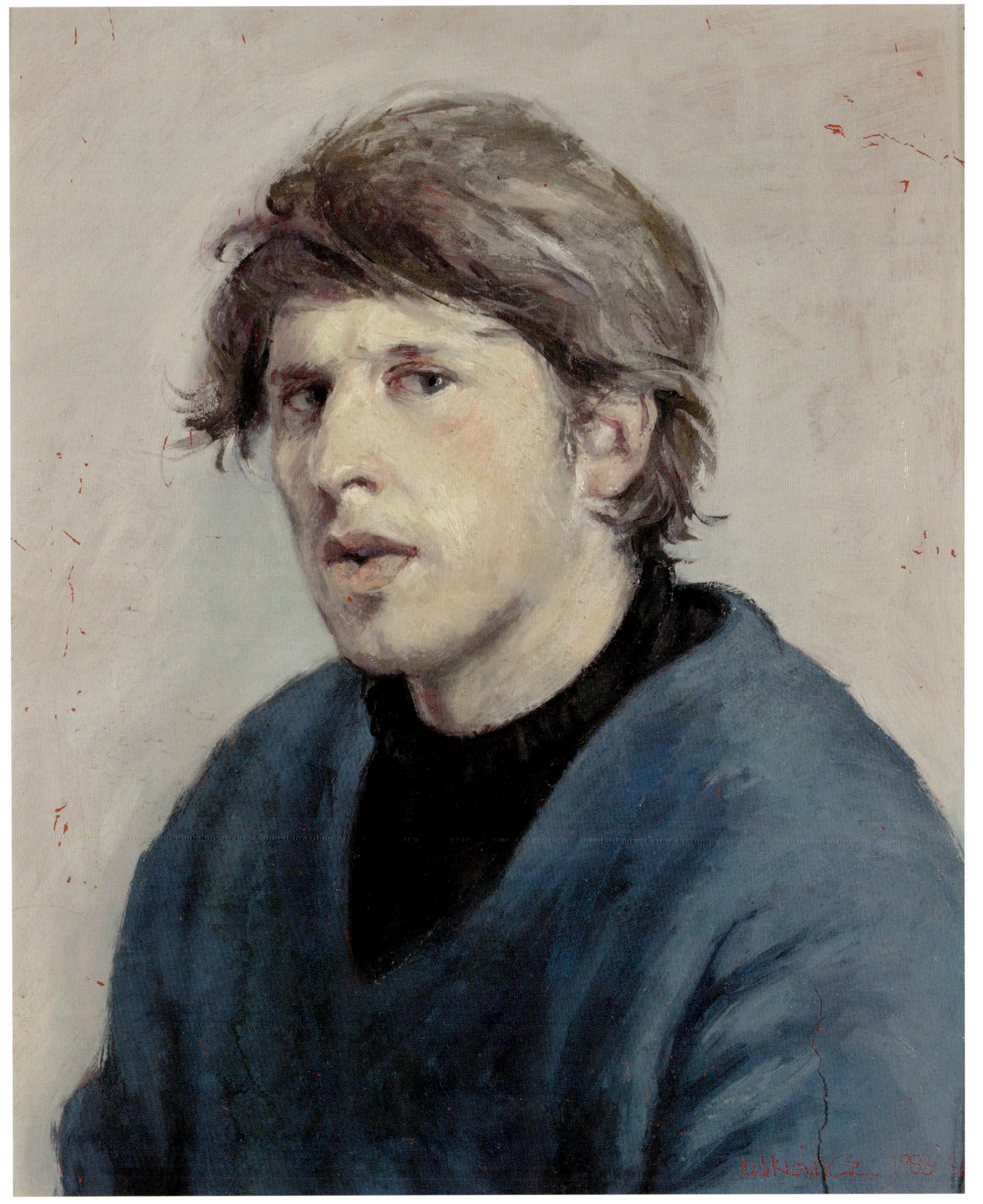

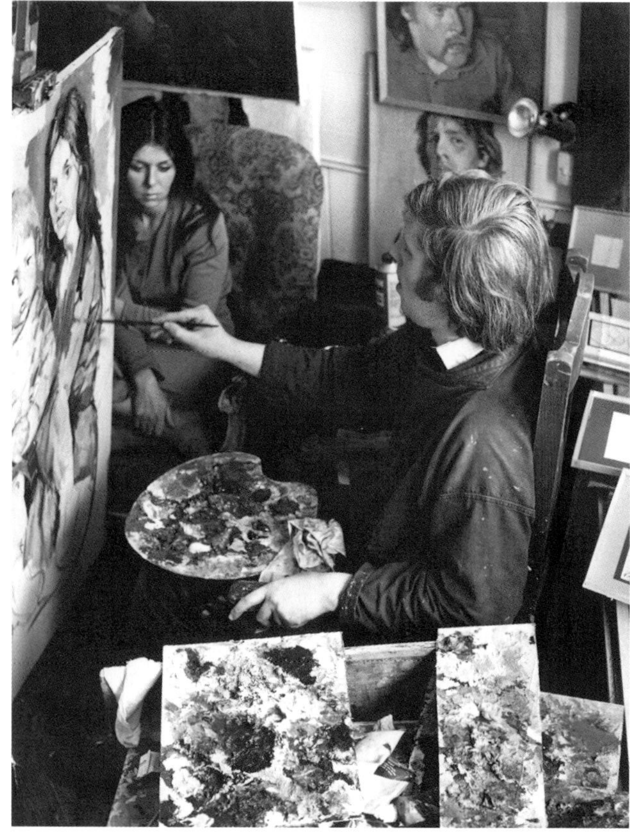

Robert Lenkiewicz painting Monica Quirk and their son Reuben in The Portrait Painter studio at No. 25 The Parade, 1970.
Photo: courtesy of M. Quirk.

*c.*1968
Self-Portrait.
Oil on board.
55 x 45 cm.

Mouse: There would be vagrants in the bathroom, under the stairs, in the airing cupboards … it was so noisy; we had The Beatles on full pelt. Imagine living next to us; it must have been unbearable!

Monica: It was an eccentric house. But these weren't young homeless people – they were elderly men who had lived rough a long time, plus one woman; dear old Winnie. We were all very idealistic …

Mouse: … and brainwashed!

Monica: Apart from doing his painting Robert would do lots and lots of drawings and little paintings and we'd go round and flog them locally.

Mouse: But we were *so-o* poor! We'd go to the shop and buy two fags.

Monica: Robert would take drawings to the shop and exchange them for huge bags of potatoes for soups or boxes of cereal. Once he had the downstairs shop in Clifton Street, called The Fool, tramps came from far and wide. They knew he was a soft touch – no sooner had Robert made a tenner than they'd be lining up for a handout. He was sentimentally generous at times – he could just give you a painting on a whim. But sometimes you might be desperate for a little money, for a child's shoes or something, and he could be like Richard the Third – 'Thou troublest me; I am not in the vein!'

Mouse: He completely pleased himself with no guilt about trying to please anyone else. The only time he would ever put himself out was to win a woman [laughs]! He *was* selfish, but incredibly kind and generous too at times.

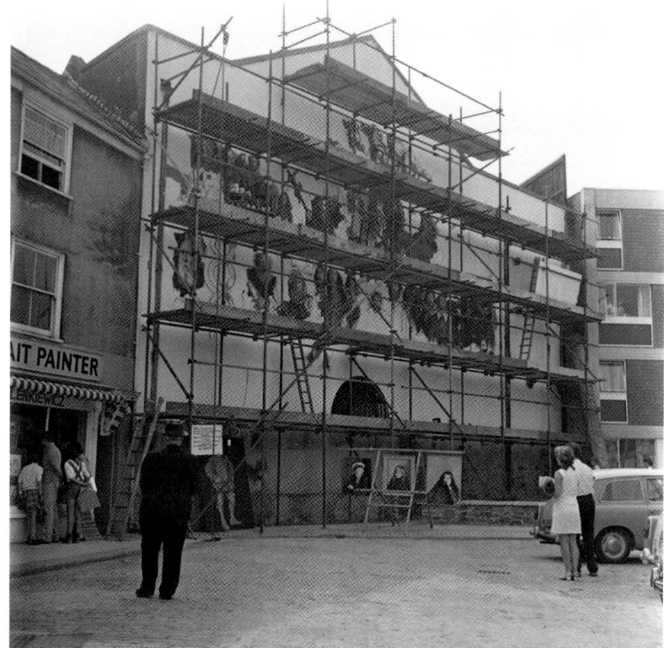

Setting out his stall: Lenkiewicz opens The Portrait Painter at No. 25 The Parade and begins work on the Barbican Mural in 1971.
Photo: Southwest Image Bank.

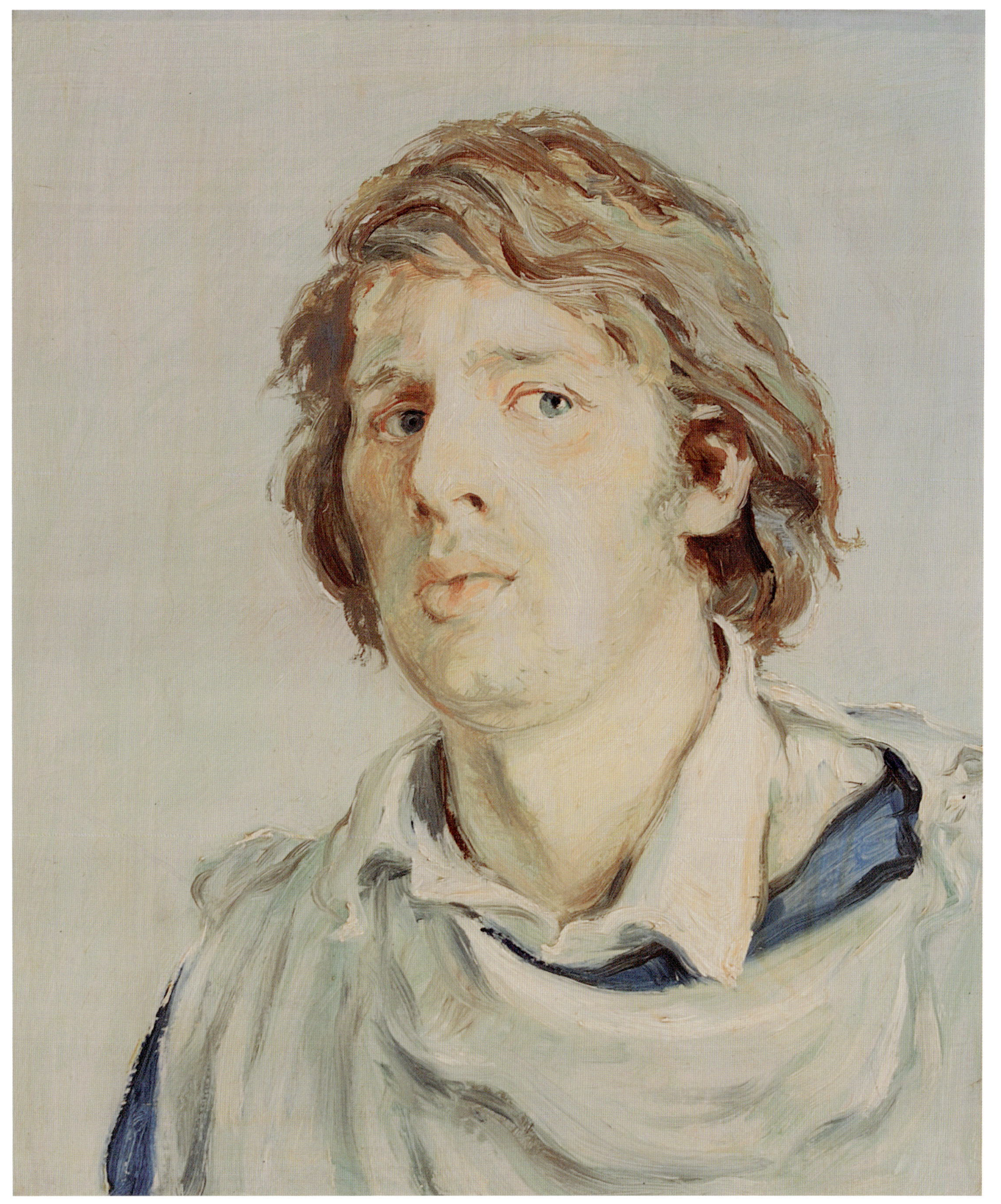

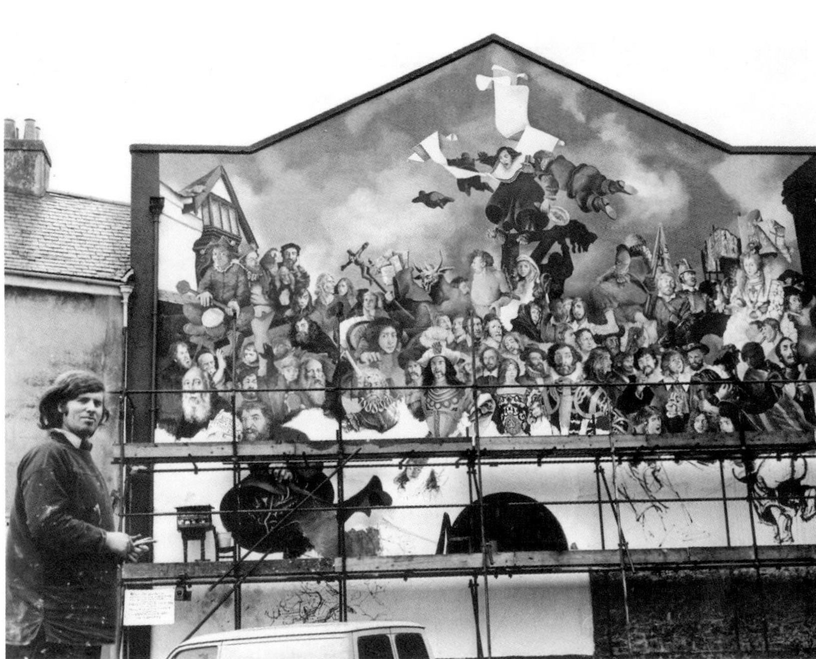

The *Barbican Mural* nears completion in 1972. At 3000 sq. ft in size, it is titled *The Influence of Jewish Thought on Elizabethan Culture, 1580-1620.*
Photo: Southwest Image Bank.

"It is intended that the Barbican Mural *should convey some feeling of the demoniac brilliance of the Elizabethan Age, a time of great skills, flights of imagination, and great brutalities, a time very much like our own."*

R.O. Lenkiewicz
Notes on the Barbican Mural, 1972

1973
The Painter With Diogenes.
Cryla on masonite.
84 x 77 cm.
Inscribed: Fragment of The Hoe Theatre Mural,
from Commedia dell'arte Theme.

Robert Lenkiewicz: A Plymothian's Perspective
Chris Robinson

For the wider public Lenkiewicz arrived in the city as some kind of free-thinking, post-hippy portrait painter, whose early portraits often echoed his own features, even when he wasn't painting himself: fulsome mouths with eyes wide open. However, with the completion of his massive *Barbican Mural* and other large scale works around the city, his reputation grew, as did the quality of his craftsmanship and the demand for his work.

The bigger canvasses and the greater degree of attention also unlocked the potential of yet more mischief making. A mural painted on the walls of the erstwhile Civic Theatre on Plymouth Hoe depicted, in the words of the artist: 'a history of the Harlequinade from about 1580 to about 1860, a survey of the Italian Commedia dell'arte.' He added: 'As usual, I selected models who live locally to represent various characters in the Harlequinade.'

Amongst those models was Edwin MacKenzie, one of Robert's favourite down-and-outs, a dosser whom he found living in a circular container overlooking the city dump at Chelson Meadow, and whom he rechristened Diogenes, in honour of the Greek philosopher who lived in a barrel. And then, inevitably, there was Robert himself. Robert's self-portrait depicted him blowing a raspberry, with Diogenes alongside him flicking a V-sign. A small part of the overall work, it nonetheless was quickly blown out of proportion; 'The mural shows people putting out their tongues and using Churchillian gestures,' complained Councillor Brian Rabin at a Junior Chamber of Commerce meeting in 1976. 'We should try and get it white-washed and restored to order. It's our theatre and this is just an obscene gesture to the people of Plymouth. And when will it be finished? We should invite vandals to come and scrawl on it.' In response Robert said he was quite willing to complete the work 'as soon as I have the time.'

Time, however, was always an issue for Robert and at the end of his life there were hundreds, perhaps thousands, of unfinished paintings. For all that though, few people I know ever made as much use of the time allotted to them as he did. In his hedonistic lifestyle doing nothing was seldom an option; he painted, he talked, he read, he wrote, he made love, and he painted some more. He slept but a few hours each night, burning the candle at both ends, extracting as much as he could from every waking moment. Around the Barbican, he traded food for paintings at his chosen, simple eateries – but notably not pubs. Joe Prete's Café and Captain Jasper's both had murals that had been

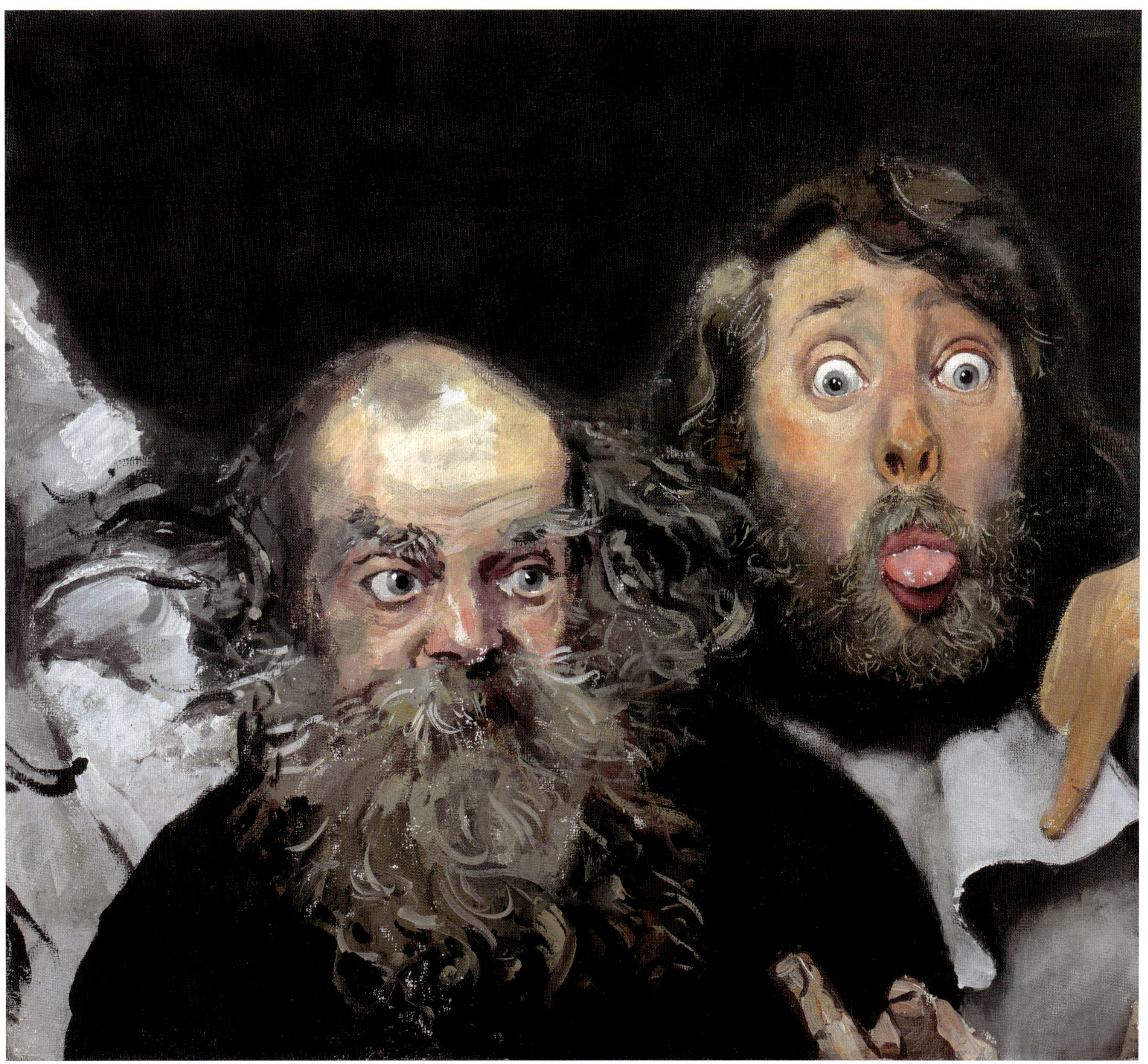

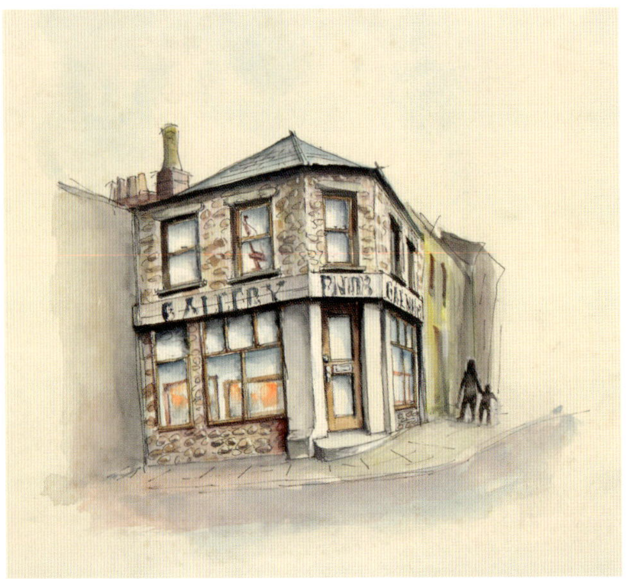

The Fool gallery in Clifton Street, illustrated here by Lenkiewicz as the Pnoob Gallery, 1974.

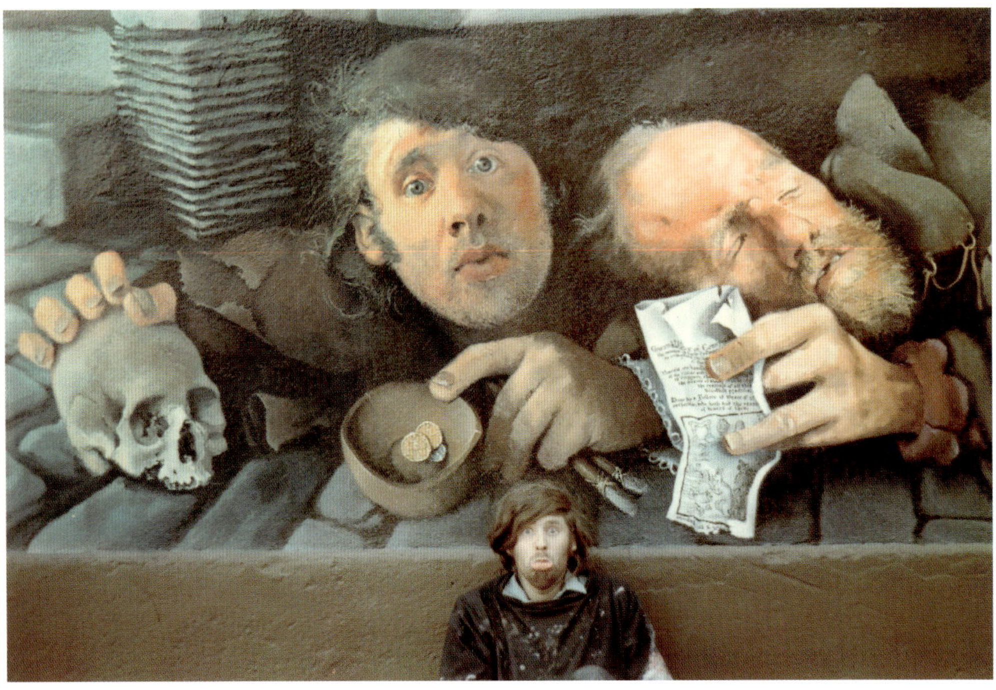

Robert makes his 'Pnoob' face in front of his self-portrait in the *Barbican Mural* in 1973.
Pnoob is the innocent fictional hero of Robert's children's book *The Quest of Pnoob*, which exists only as a richly illustrated manuscript. *Photo*: courtesy of N. Shoa.

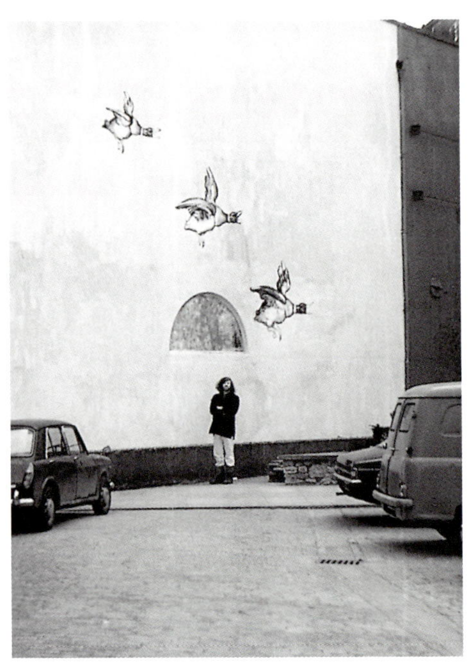

Democratic taste: the *Barbican Mural* repainted on 1 April 1981. *Photo:* collection of the artist.

swapped for seemingly limitless supplies of burgers and other, not desperately healthy, fast food and Robert could regularly be seen patronising both establishments.

However, despite a lifestyle that would take a toll on many mortals, no one, apart from Robert himself, anticipated the news of his sudden death in London in February 1981. Just a week earlier Robert had asked that the proceeds from his latest exhibition at 25 The Parade – 'Still-Lives and Other Works' – be given to the neighbouring Plymouth Age Concern Centre on The Barbican. 'He was tremendously interested in our work and spoke brilliantly at our conferences,' said the charity's chairman Elspeth Sitters.

In the event, the 39-year-old Robert 'still-lives' Lenkiewicz dominated the front page of the local papers for three days and, on the third day, described the event, which he refused to acknowledge as a hoax, as a 'three-tiered resurrection cake'. The first tier was a variation on the theme of being dead; the second was a sincere wish to indirectly benefit Plymouth Age Concern, while the third tier was of 'an intimate and private nature and could not be discussed'. Dismissing claims that he had done it for money, Robert suggested, with more *gravitas* than people perhaps perceived at the time, that by reappearing he had proved that he was 'not a financial wizard'. He added: 'My work is valueless, dead or alive.'

Not surprisingly the local press had a field day. Previously critical councillors had sung the praises of the 'dead' man, and calls for a memorial had been made, while *The Western Evening Herald* claimed that they never believed the story in the first place. The *Sunday Independent* put journalist Jim Dalrymple on the case and his verdict, although by no means a universal one, was:

'Robert is a self-publicist in the heavyweight division, a kind of Barnum and Bailey of the art world … Since he came to staid old Plymouth more than a decade ago and proceeded to turn the place on its head, redesign it to his vision and entertain us all hugely, he has courted the media as ardently as any public relations man … A lot of people are going to be angry at Robert for his little performance last week. Nobody, not even your best friend, likes delivering eulogies to a corpse that suddenly jumps up and grins. But they'll forgive him. Plymouth will welcome him home with open arms. Because without Lenkiewicz the city would have been that much poorer. Nice one Robert.'

Certainly there were a few angry people around that week, some of them from the media itself, as Robert, having granted a press conference at his studio, not only kept the newspaper, television and radio journalists waiting, but also left them abruptly and locked them in while he made an early escape. A few weeks later, after the dust and death notices had settled, and doubtless partly in the wake of the city's earlier removal of the 'controversial' *Hoe Theatre Mural*, Robert's most famous public artwork, the 3000 sq. ft *Barbican Mural*, was painted over in an apparent act of vandalism. Three flying ducks, that potent symbol of horrible household 'art', had been painted over the cherished celebration of The Barbican's Elizabethan heritage.

The date of this episode in the Lenkiewicz Chronicles was 1 April 1981. It was, of course, Robert who had painted over the mural, and he had done so with a water-based whitewash that did little or no harm to the paintwork beneath it. Time, however, took its toll on that landmark work, as it has on his other, more provocative piece – the nude montage on the Southside Street elevation of 'The House that Jack Built' called *The Last Judgement*.

In the meantime what is the real legacy for Plymouth and how will Robert be remembered? 'Some people probably regard me as a deranged necrophiliac, littering the streets of Plymouth with my children,' he was once quoted as saying, in reference to the embalming of Diogenes and the dozen or so children he sired over the years. For almost forty years Lenkiewicz brought colour and life to The Barbican, his time there coinciding with the area's transformation from a down at heel historic quarter, newly rescued from plans for so-called 'slum clearance', into a vibrant and colourful community, one that would provide another much missed Plymouth-based artist, Beryl Cook, with material to delight and enchant the world of popular art.

Robert was too old school for that sort of commercial success. There's no doubting his ability: Robert was simply one of the best, and probably the most prolific, portrait painters of the twentieth century. Sadly much of the content of the studio has been dispersed in the fallout that inevitably followed his eventual – certified – death but enough remains to create a fitting memorial/museum to a man who left an impression on almost everyone who lived in his adopted city; and as time allows us to fully take stock of not just his major paintings but the vast, and largely unseen, wealth of observation contained in the masses of notebooks and illustrated diaries he left behind, it would be our loss if such a place was not to be created.

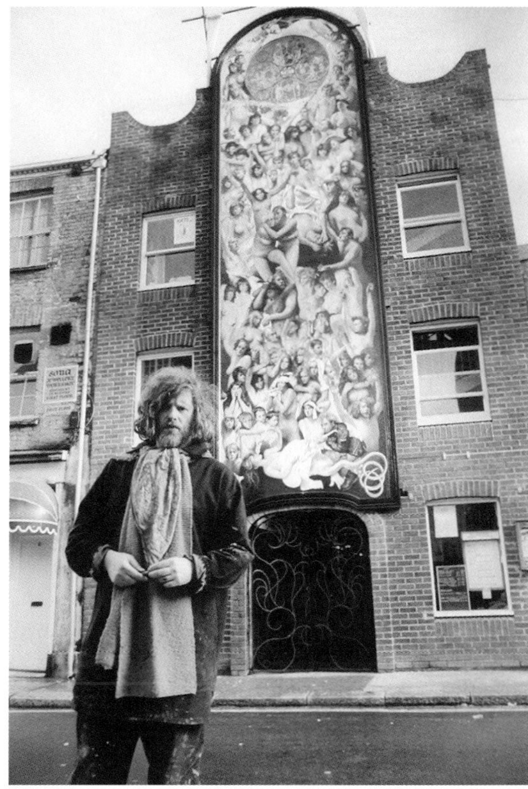

The Last Judgement Mural on The House That Jack Built in Southside Street, 1985.
Photo: Southwest Image Bank.

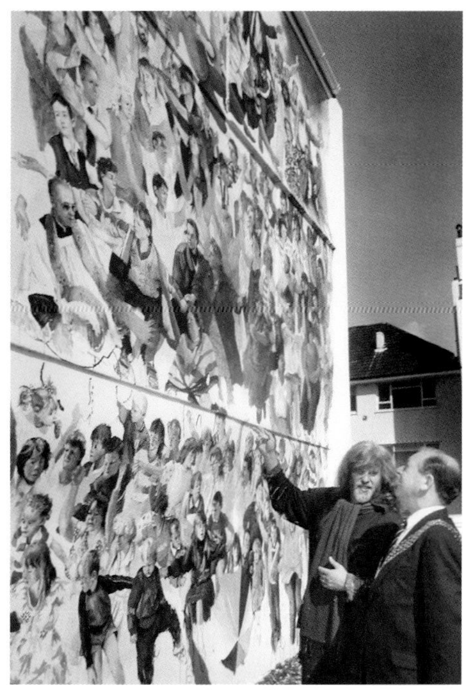

Urban renewal: The *Devonport Mural*, completed in 1988, features Dr David Owen MP and local residents. *Photo:* Southwest Image Bank.

'What you see is nothing, the head manufactures the world.

It takes a lunatic to find out what is really going on. You are now talking to a lunatic, sir! A lunatic is someone who takes an interest in something no one else takes an interest in. For the rest there is no escape.'

Albert Fisher, known as Bishop, a vagrant

'We're all vagrants in the sense that we're not here to stay.'

Terry Goldstone, political activist

'The word vagrancy is stupid; we're all human beings. It's bad to call a man a vagrant; he's a human being, that's all. I've met all kinds of people that were called vagrants: their clothing might look a bit rough, but the mind is the most important thing in the world and some of them have wonderful minds you know.'

Charles Christopher Byrne, known as The Singer

Q. Why do you consider yourself a vagrant?
A. 'Cos I'm in every bugger's way.

Edwin MacKenzie, known as Diogenes, a tramp

Observations on Local Vagrancy
published by Robert Lenkiewicz in 1973

The vagrant Albert Fisher, known as Bishop, seated in front of the 1972 canvas *Bishop Startled*. *Photo:* J.L. Bremer.

1973
Mr R. Lenkiewicz.
Oil on canvas.
80 x 60 cm.

RL: I'd break into warehouses [to house the vagrants], disused premises, put new padlocks on them and get neighbouring shops to put in an extension lead for a single light. There were nine of them. I had good relations with local hospitals and we got 170 beds, mattresses and cabinets. I had to block up all the lift shafts because when they were drunk they would have just blundered into them, and remove all the broken glass from the windows. Two or three were studios; the rest weren't suitable. There was a book at each one of the places if I wanted to record anything. It was marvellous chaos.

Their greatest strength was that they knew that nobody gave a shit and neither did they. If anyone thought they cared about them they'd take him to the cleaners. Brother Blair was the main one for that. He'd say, 'The ones I really want to get are the do-gooders: I don't believe a fuckin' word of it!'

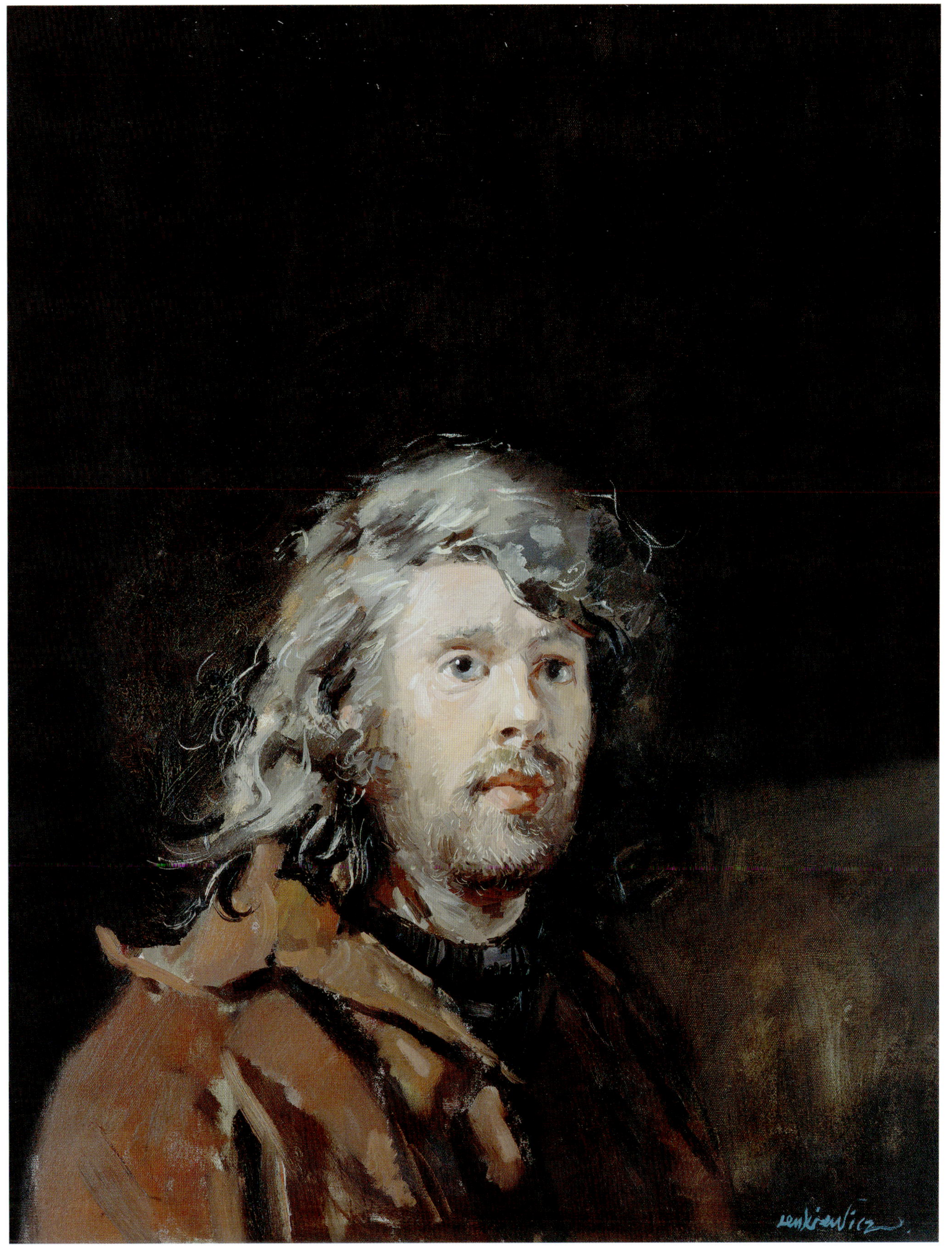

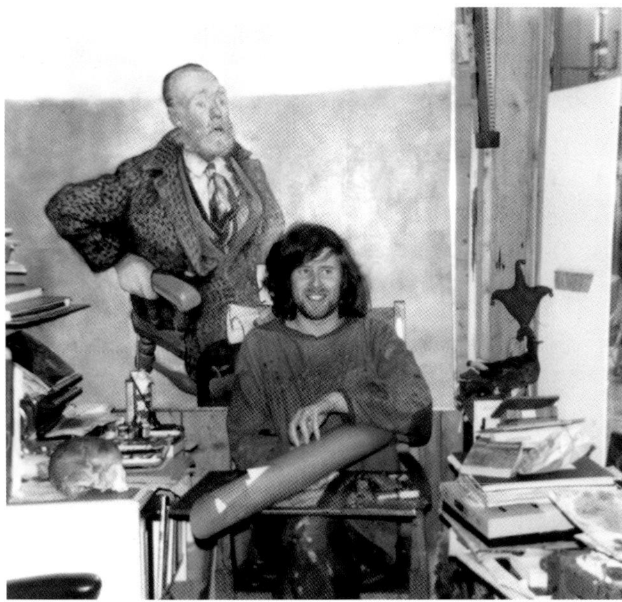

Robert Lenkiewicz in The Portrait Painter studio at No. 25 The Parade, 1973. *Photo:* J.L. Bremer.

1973
Self-Portrait Aged 32.

Oil on canvas.

46 x 30 cm.

'The innuendo of the "masterpiece" is that its creator has transcended both himself and Society; that it is in some sense, prophecy. If the item has been purchased, then we are reminded of a slave-trader wily enough to buy "good stock". Such images develop like institutions or minor religions imbued with qualities that we conspire with. The "masterpiece" can be seen as an abstracted extension of the "hero", and its function in Society operates as an amulet or talisman.'

Diogenes Con Show & The Masterpiece Museum Notebook, 1975

'I was interviewed a few years ago by the television for something or other … so I put Mary on my lap and began painting a portrait of her and myself, in a mirror, and started *spieling* away at the same time about the commercial assumption that a painted image has got more significance, more heart and soul, more ethos under each layer of paint, than a photograph. I said, why should this be the case? If I had the choice between a fantasy portrait of Jesus and a black and white passport photograph of him, I know which I'd prefer … I ended up with the John Berger remark: do people really believe Velázquez painted a king's head with a different state of mind from painting a peasant's arse?'

R.O. Lenkiewicz
Philip Stokes Notebooks, vol. 2, April 1984

RL: There were two exhibitions running parallel with each other. One was called *The Masterpiece Museum* and the other one was called the *Diogenes Con Show*. It was an ironic investigation into art and commerce, and it was just a short, small exhibition which I staged for a brief period of time. However, it did actually end up in Piccadilly; I can't remember quite why or how. There were two rooms: one room had a long red carpet with the 'Masterpiece' on the wall, which actually was *Plymouth Mourning Over its Unfortunates*. It was in a very dimly lit room, with dark brown walls, and all along the walls were hung all the designs, sketches and studies for a build-up towards this 'Masterpiece' which stood on the red carpet. There was a special chain all the way around, and somebody in uniform seated in the corner.

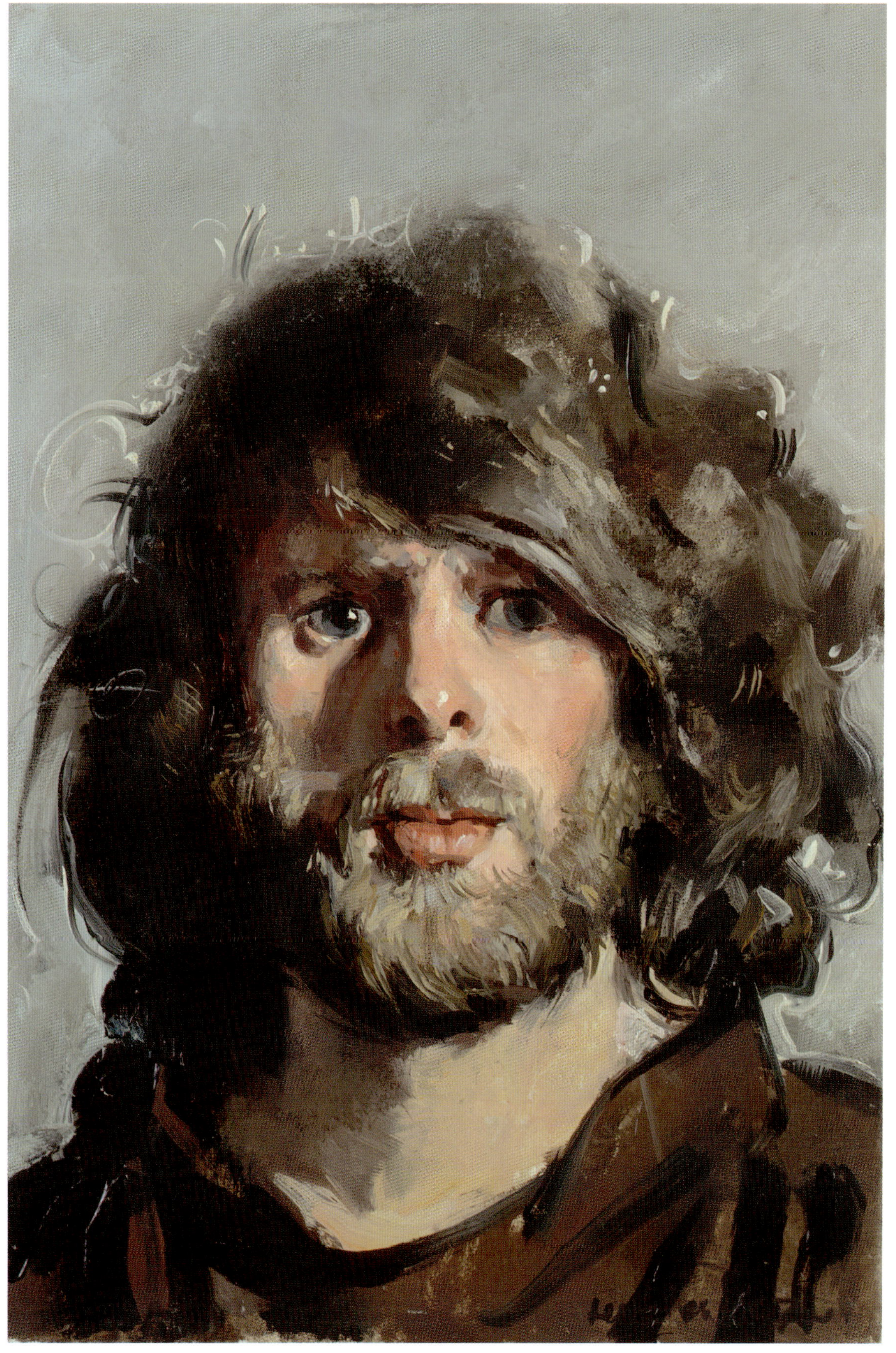

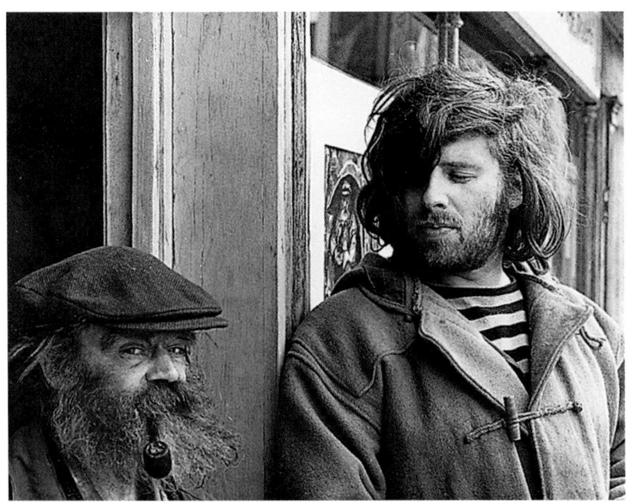

Thirty-five studies of Diogenes, with titles like *This Study Took 23 Minutes*, made up the *Diogenes Con Show*, shown at The Fool and then at the Blenheim Gallery, London.
Photo: Southwest Image Bank.

"One clear distinction between the 'image' of Diogenes – philosopher–rogue and Diogenes – Edwin MacKenzie in the real world is that the 'image' of him is far more acceptable in the average household than the man himself."

R.O. Lenkiewicz
Diogenes Con Show & The Masterpiece Museum Notebook, 1975

1974
The Painter With Courbet's Self-Portrait.
Oil on canvas.
121 x 76 cm.

R.O. LENKIEWICZ
PAINTINGS
May 6 to June 20 1975
Blenheim Gallery, 21 Cork Street, W1

NOTE
Amusing or not, the present exhibition is a joke. It is hoped that those who profess an interest will take the trouble to read the leaflets that accompany the collection.

THE MASTERPIECE MUSEUM
The gallery has experimented with a small display of the work of a now forgotten painter.

Some attention should be drawn towards the manuscript cabinet which contains a few very rare examples of the painter's numberless sketchbooks.

We are grateful to the Plymouth Archives for the loan of these items. The remainder were unfortunately stolen from the museum by an irresponsible art student some years ago. An added attraction is the collection of miscellaneous pieces in the tall cabinet near the entrance. Of special interest is the article on *The Uses of Bad Art* by Geoffrey Grigson. It is said that the painter died with this paper clutched to his heart.

There are no 'last words' recorded of this strange man: though it is significant that an envelope filled with cuttings and quotations of famous last words, was after found beneath his pillow. In the cabinet can be seen a feeble scrawl on blue paper (one of many in the envelope) which says:

'I have as my guarantee the hatred I bear towards men and towards our society, which will last as long as I live.' (Courbet to Bruyas, 1854).

This blue scrap was underlined and on the floor; it would not be over-imaginative to speculate that this indeed was the intended 'last word' of our hero.

R.O. Lenkiewicz
Diogenes Con Show & The Masterpiece Museum Exhibition Notes, 1975

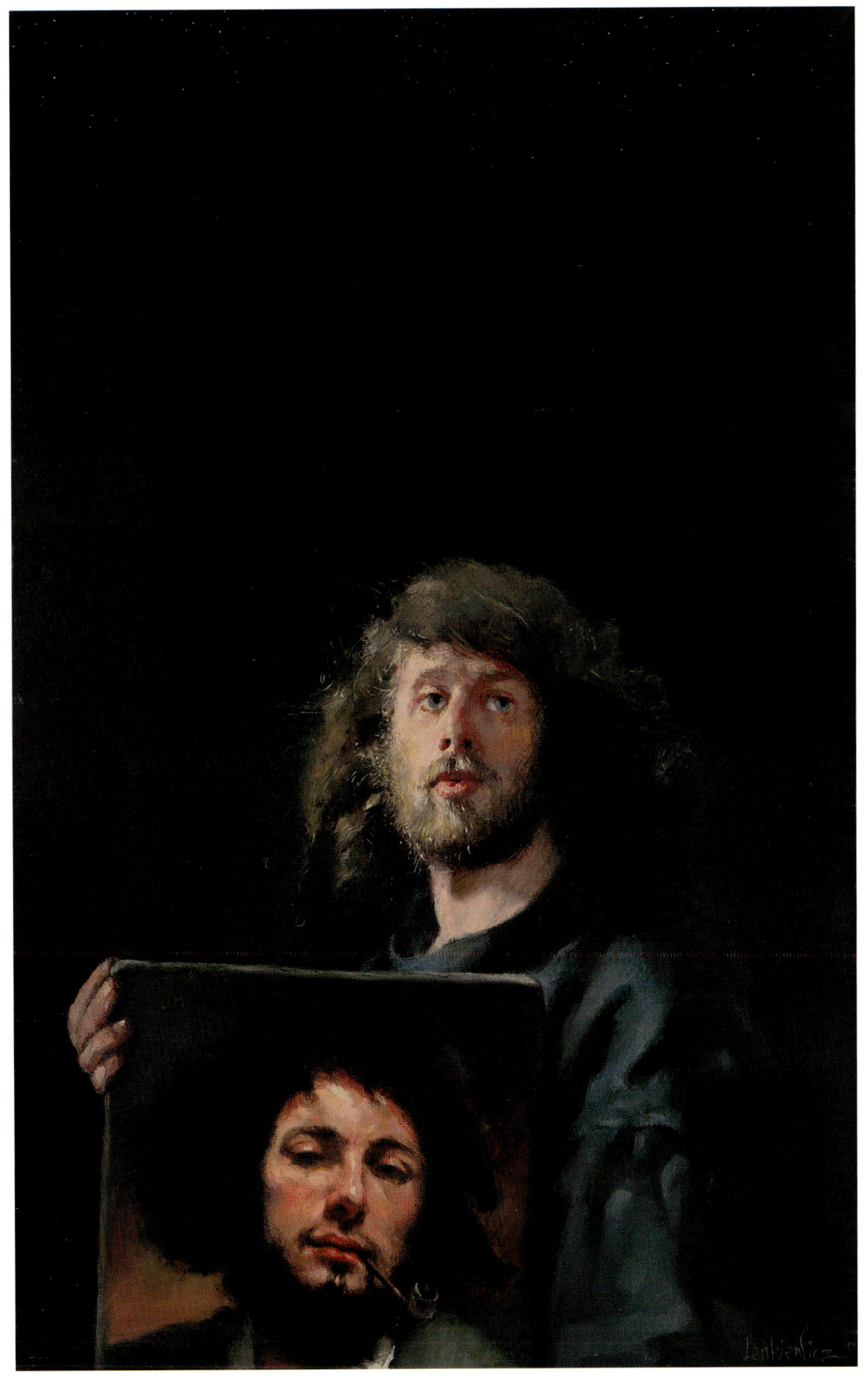

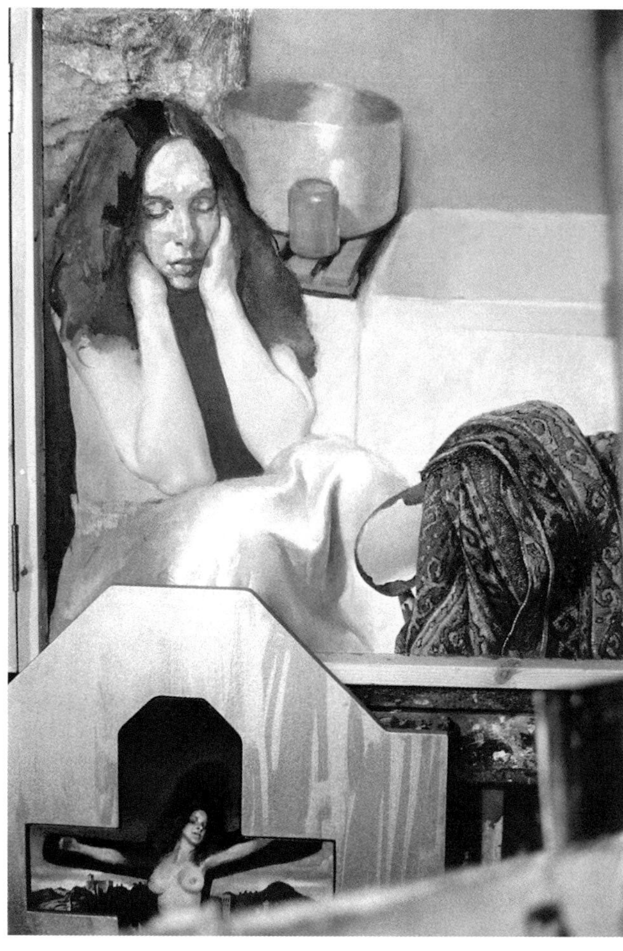

The *Love & Romance Theme* imagery: portrait of Annie Hill-Smith on the theme of 'Pot with Human Still-Life'. The smaller, framed painting is *Belle with Mantegna's Dead Christ in Bellini's Landscape* (1975). *Photo:* Dr P. Stokes.

1975

Self-Portrait With Monica (diptych).

Oil on panel.

36 x 23 cm. (left panel of diptych).

'An unrequited energy is the lifeblood of creativity.'

R.O. Lenkiewicz
Retrospective: *Plymouth City Museum & Art Gallery, 1997*

'We are told of two thieves who hang by the side of a crucified man (in romantic love, there are two thieves constantly stealing from each other, who finally crucify each other). We are further told of the Deposition, when the dead man is brought down from the cross and mourned (in romantic love, one partner grieves after the lost affections of the other). We are finally told that the dead man was resurrected (in romantic love, the "loser" in the attachment replaces the addiction with a new companion).'

R.O. Lenkiewicz
Love & Romance Notebook, 1974

'New mediocrities can haunt the mind more deeply than old profundities.'

R.O. Lenkiewicz

Monica: Robert had a number of eureka! moments in his life. I think that he realised that he did not have to live with one woman and have children. He had already done that: he had Dorian, Alice, Wolfe and Reuben. He could then say to his models 'OK, we can have a relationship but I don't live with anybody'.

Mouse: He used to say – 'I look forward to the day when the European Court of Human Rights makes it an imprisonable offence to live with another human being for more than a fortnight!'

Monica: He did, but the women didn't pay any attention. It's like someone who falls in love with an alcoholic: they think, 'I can change him.' It takes a while to realise they can't.

Mouse: Robert only really fell in love with what he couldn't have. As soon as he got that full measure of devotion he wasn't interested. I understand it completely: I do it myself; it doesn't matter how old you are, your eyes are still pleased.

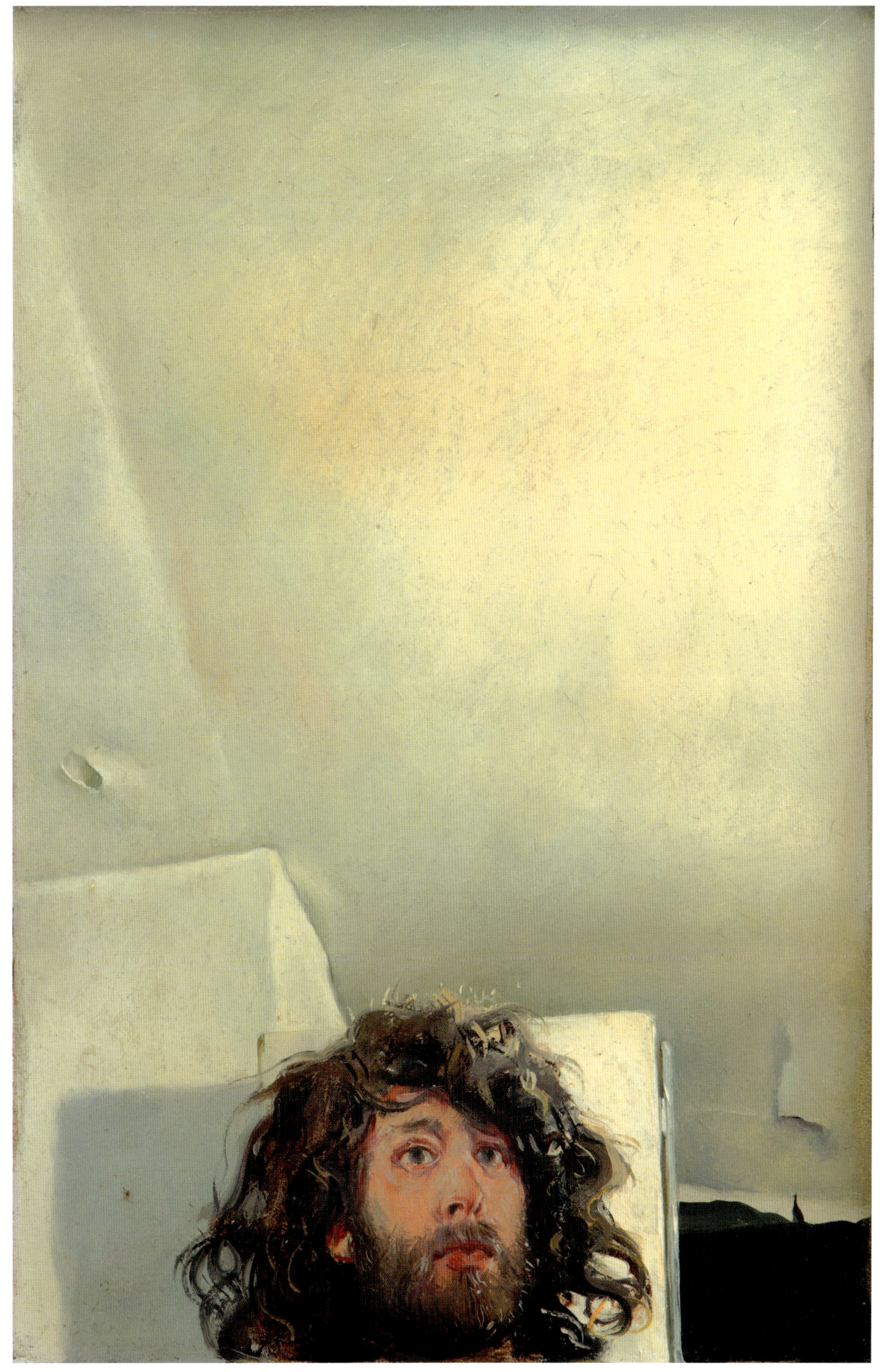

Love & Mediocrity

Nahem Shoa

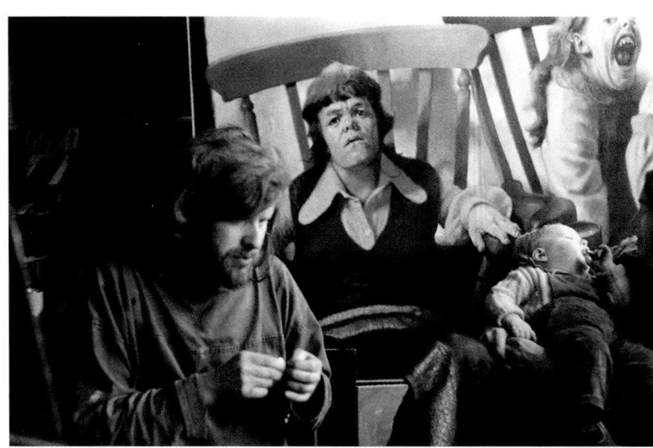

Robert with Annie Hill-Smith holding their first child, Sholem, in 1976. The canvas seen behind is *Barbara Bridgeman & Carol Young*, shown in the *Mental Handicap Project* that year at Jacob's Ladder. *Photo:* Dr P. Stokes.

1976
You Offer Me a Dead Rose, May I Give You a Dead Rat?
Oil on board.
41 x 56 cm.

Robert was on one of his visits to stay a few days with my family in west London in 1976 when we found a dead rat in the basement of our house. It wasn't a shocking sight, as in that summer our house had been plagued by them, so much so that we even had our family photo on the front cover of the *Paddington Gazette*. I remember Robert asking my father if he could have the rat to use in a self-portrait. Later on that day I recall my father taking us on a trip somewhere out of London. and when we came back in the evening the painting was finished. Apart from the self-portrait on the *Barbican Mural*, it is probably this self-portrait of Lenkiewicz' that is etched in my earliest childhood memory. Robert eating a rat appealed to my childhood imagination, which was filled with stories of Sinbad, the Greek myths, ogres and films like *King Kong*. It is a painting that seems to sum up for me Robert's life at the time in Plymouth: his monstrous vitality and awe-inspiring talent. I can still recall on my childhood visits to see Robert the aroma of the tramps, pisspots and vomit, as well as turps and oil paint, his rare books, freezing studios and vast numbers of beautiful women.

You Offer Me a Dead Rose, May I Offer You a Dead Rat? was one of the few images in his fifth project *Love & Mediocrity* which was painted directly from life rather than in the 'private language' allegorical style he mainly deployed in this project. The exhibition was staged in The Fool, his gallery in Clifton Street in Plymouth. It was part of a series of four projects, starting in 1974 with *Death and the Maiden, Love and Romance* (1975), *Love & Mediocrity* (1976) and *Jealousy* (1977), whose themes were more subjective in nature. Lenkiewicz began using material from his own relationships with women to study the physiology of 'falling in love' and the lover's dependence on another person. Many of the ideas behind the paintings in these projects dealt with the theme of love or the falling-in-love process and the consequences of the breakdown of a relationship, which he saw as a kind of putrefaction, aptly illustrated by the dead rat, a medieval symbol of decay and the passing of time. This also linked to the fourteenth- and fifteenth-century association of erotic passion with decay, succinctly conveyed by Saint Augustine's quote that Lenkiewicz often used – 'The body's pleasure areas are also the body's sewers'.

There is also a more humorous side to this painting that reminds me of the great nineteenth-century animal painter Edwin Landseer and his paintings of a dog bringing in a dead-animal offering to its master, which it has just gleefully killed. Lenkiewicz's self-portrait has the same sheepish stare, a mixture between vulnerability and brute strength. Of course, he would also have been haunted by darker images such as Goya's and Ruben's paintings of the god Saturn eating his own children. I am also reminded of the similarity between his dead rat self-portrait and Lucian Freud's startling *Naked Man with Rat*, painted a year later, where the rat's tail almost strokes the red-headed man's penis. I know this naked portrait was one of three or four images of Freud's that Lenkiewicz most admired as a tour de force of the realisation of flesh in paint. Similarly to Freud,

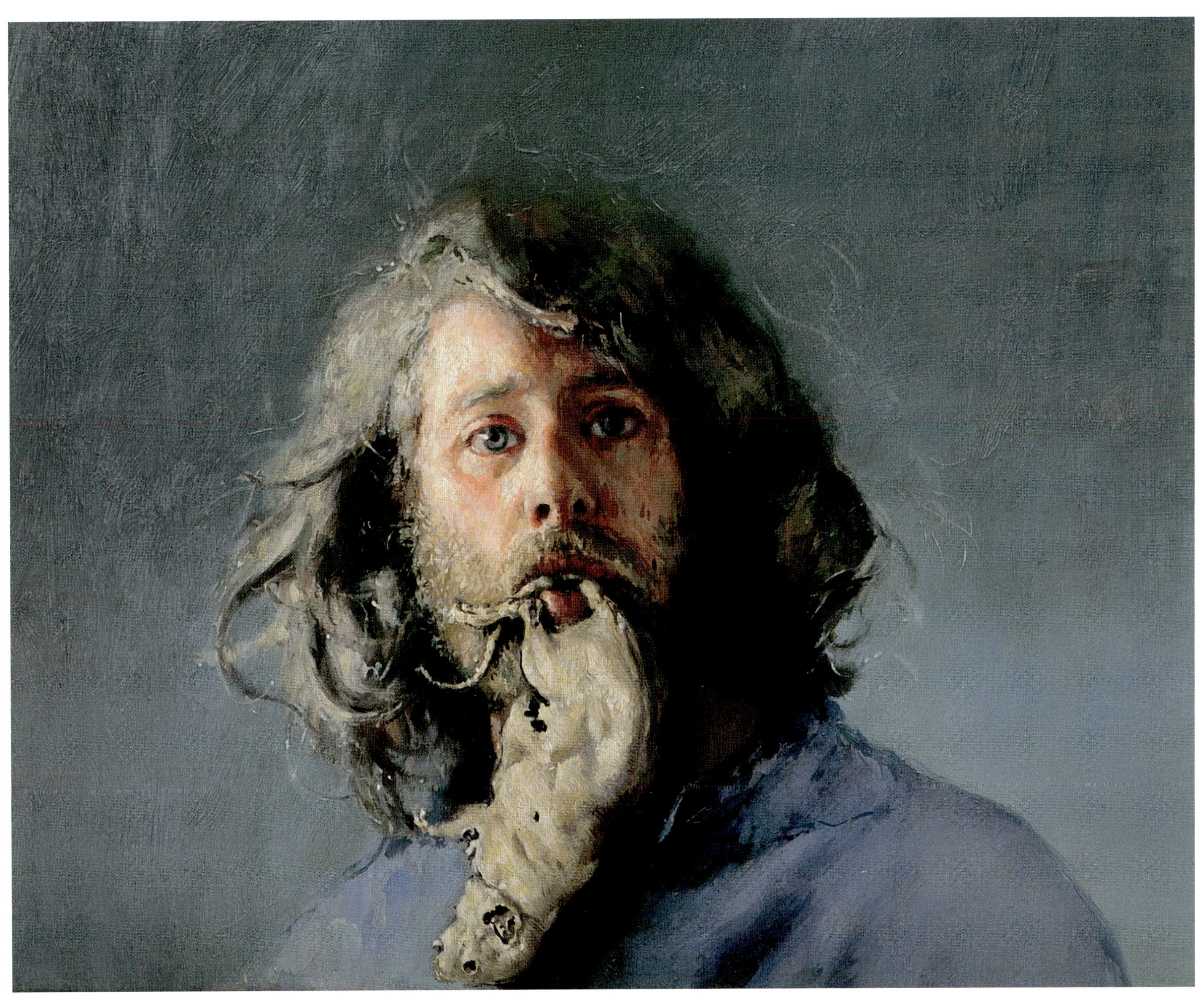

Lenkiewicz had the ability to endow each brushstroke with living form and boundless life-energy.

This self-portrait is painted at the tail end of what I've always seen as Lenkiewicz's 'Frans Hals period' of the early to middle 1970s – paintings defined by swashbuckling brushstrokes, driven around the canvas at breakneck speed, but all held together by his sharpness of eye, scrupulously exact tones and dynamic draughtsmanship. During this period Lenkiewicz would often paint two of three portraits in one session in some manic competition with himself and the great painters of the past. Often he utilised a seventeenth-century Dutch palette of reddish-brown warm shadow tones, cooled a little by terre verte green and black, adding orange-brown in the mid-tones and yellow highlights – though sometimes he would also paint with cooler earth colours, using a combination of blue, green and brown on subtle black backgrounds.

A lifetime of being in the business of capturing the appearance of human form had given Lenkiewicz's expressive handling of paint the look of flesh and blood. The warmer red-orange tones of the head are wonderfully brought out by the deep mid-tone background made up of green-blue with a hint of cadmium red in order to neutralise subtly the green. Set against this rich silky-blue background, the blackish-brown dark of the hair gives the portrait a powerful sense of animation and life, in direct contrast to the sickly ochre and terre verte of the rotting rat. The light blue-green shoulder next to the rat's head blends into the background, allowing the sharp focus of the putrefied beast's outline to affront the attention of the spectator. Flicks, blobs, scratches and smudges work together to create a remarkably alive picture surface. The best portraits from this time onwards demonstrate that Lenkiewicz had found his own profoundly modern language and way of rendering his sensations and ideas into paint. After the shock of looking at this portrait again, I am amazed by the absolute right-ness of each passage of tone and his penetrating ability to render the exact optical impression in front of his gaze.

I see this work as a turning point in terms of his painterly language, moving in approach towards a deeper understanding of the breakdown of light through vivid colour and more airy tones. In 1978 he painted two mesmerising self-portraits, directly inspired by Dürer's famous self-portrait as Christ. Like Dürer, the modelling of form in both these heads is rendered in microscopic detail. By 1980 Lenkiewicz had managed to escape the last remnants of the Hals and Dürer influences on his work and had begun to move away from a Northern European tradition. This broader, more impressionistic approach involved no preliminary drawing, but used his 'shape of the shape, tone of the tone and colour of the colour' formula to capture the event direct from life. He used to call this approach to painting 'seeing the whole'.

1978
Self-Portrait.
Oil on canvas.
46 x 92 cm.

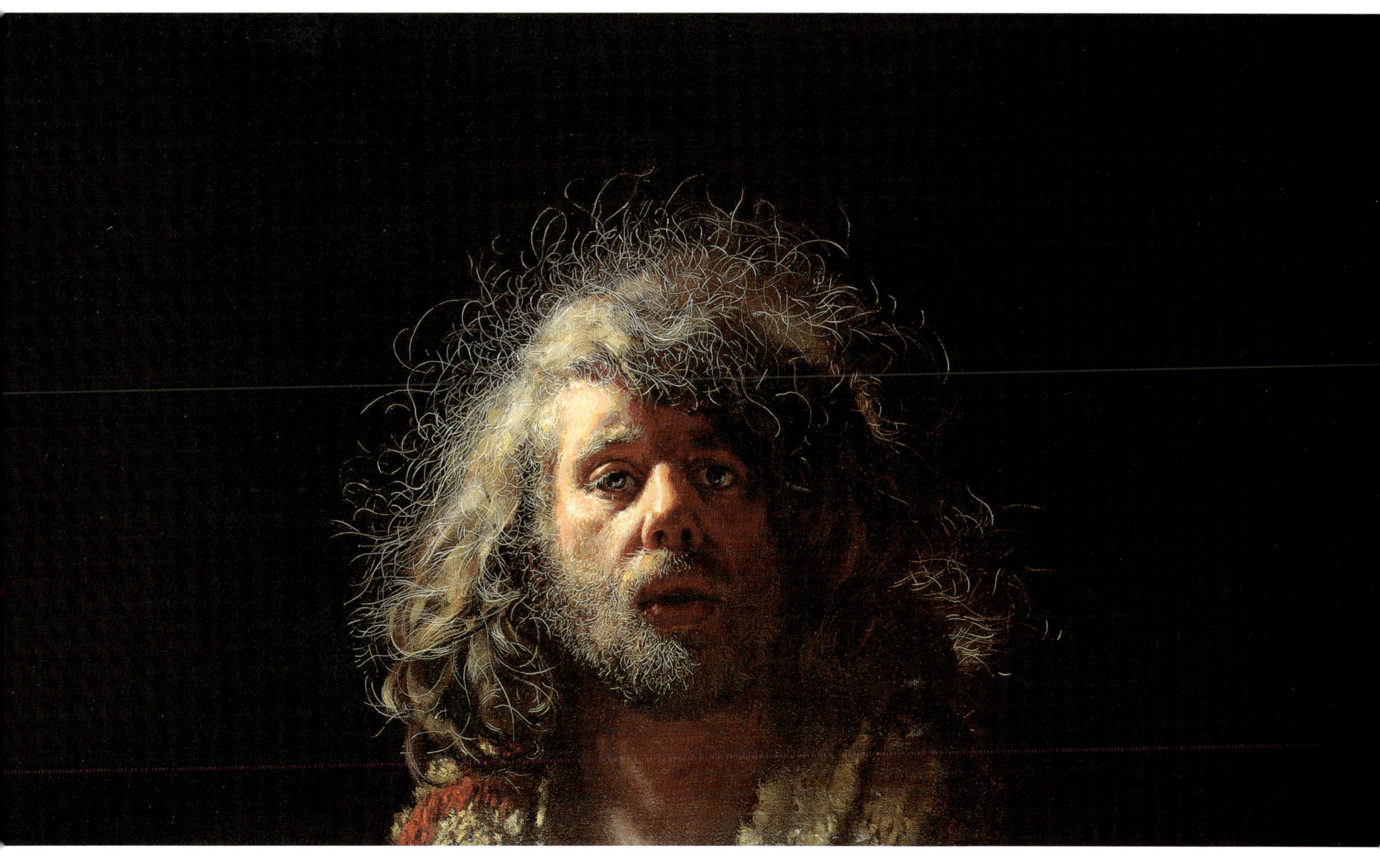

The studio at No. 25 The Parade in 1979. The *Jealousy Theme* painting *Man Watching Woman Walk Away*, painted in 1977, is seen top right. *Photo:* Dr P. Stokes.

1978

Self-Portrait With Mephistopheles.

Oil on board.

102 x 61 cm.

On Self-Portrait

R.O. Lenkiewicz

'When we try to examine the mirror in itself we discover in the end nothing but things upon it. If we want to grasp the things we finally get hold of nothing but the mirror. This, in the most general terms, is the history of knowledge.'

Friedrich Nietzsche
Daybreak: Thoughts on the Prejudices of Morality
trans. R.J. Hollingdale (Cambridge, 1982), p. 141

'Accessories should play the same role in a picture as confidants do in tragedies'.

D. Ingres

The 'self-portrait,' both visible and invisible. The portrait, the sitter and the mirror are perfect likenesses of each other, although no one can say which one conferred its likeness on the other. The mirror – the invisible guest – has been eluded, conjured away. The portrait of the painter by himself, for seven centuries from manuscript margin to the black nights of the future where self-images will spread across galaxies. Portrait of the painter by himself 1450, 1498, 1527, 1538, 1564, 1587, 1606, 1634, 1638, 1783, 1787, 1824, 1918, 1954, 1988. The names change: Lippi, Raphael, Bandinelli, Rubens, Rembrandt, Gauguin, Mondrian, Man Ray. Is the self-portrait of a mirror? Which mirror is it that poses for the portrait?

The self-portrait may be the recurrent portrait of Narcissus, a monotonous repetition. Did Apelles never portray himself? Did Phidias bequeath his likeness? Did Archedemos of Thera? Pausanias, Pliny and Boccaccio declare they did. But Tiepolo was to paint himself as Apelles, Rembrandt as Zeuxis, and in 1827 Ingres painted Apelles as Raphael's guide. Their absence was to remain an obsession. The painter advances from the margin of manuscripts to the borders of frescoes and altarpieces. One painter wears a certain type of cap, another wears a dark ribbon round his wrist. Yet another parts his hair in the middle. There are those who surround themselves with miscellaneous objects scattered about the painted space; and not one of the objects is neutral. The costume, the written words, the attitude, none of these is a matter of chance. It is all cipher, bearing the seal of identity. Cézanne painting Cézanne is painting more a Cézanne than a portrait of Cézanne, whereas the portrait of Dürer is first and foremost a portrait of Dürer before it is a Dürer by Dürer. Which of the two, Dürer or Cézanne, speaks more of painting? The portrait of the painter by himself is dual: it is of and by; it concerns the identity of the painter and is about painting. Which comes first? The painter painting himself looks in a mirror at the model he constitutes and it is the mirror that he paints. The painter paints the viewer, the person is looking at himself. When the mirror is eluded, the portrait looks at me. What the portrait of the painter by himself reveals is the look itself; and what it reveals belongs to an entirely different sphere, that of narratives and anecdotes. In the same way as the reconstruction of a crime may tell us nothing of the motive, a

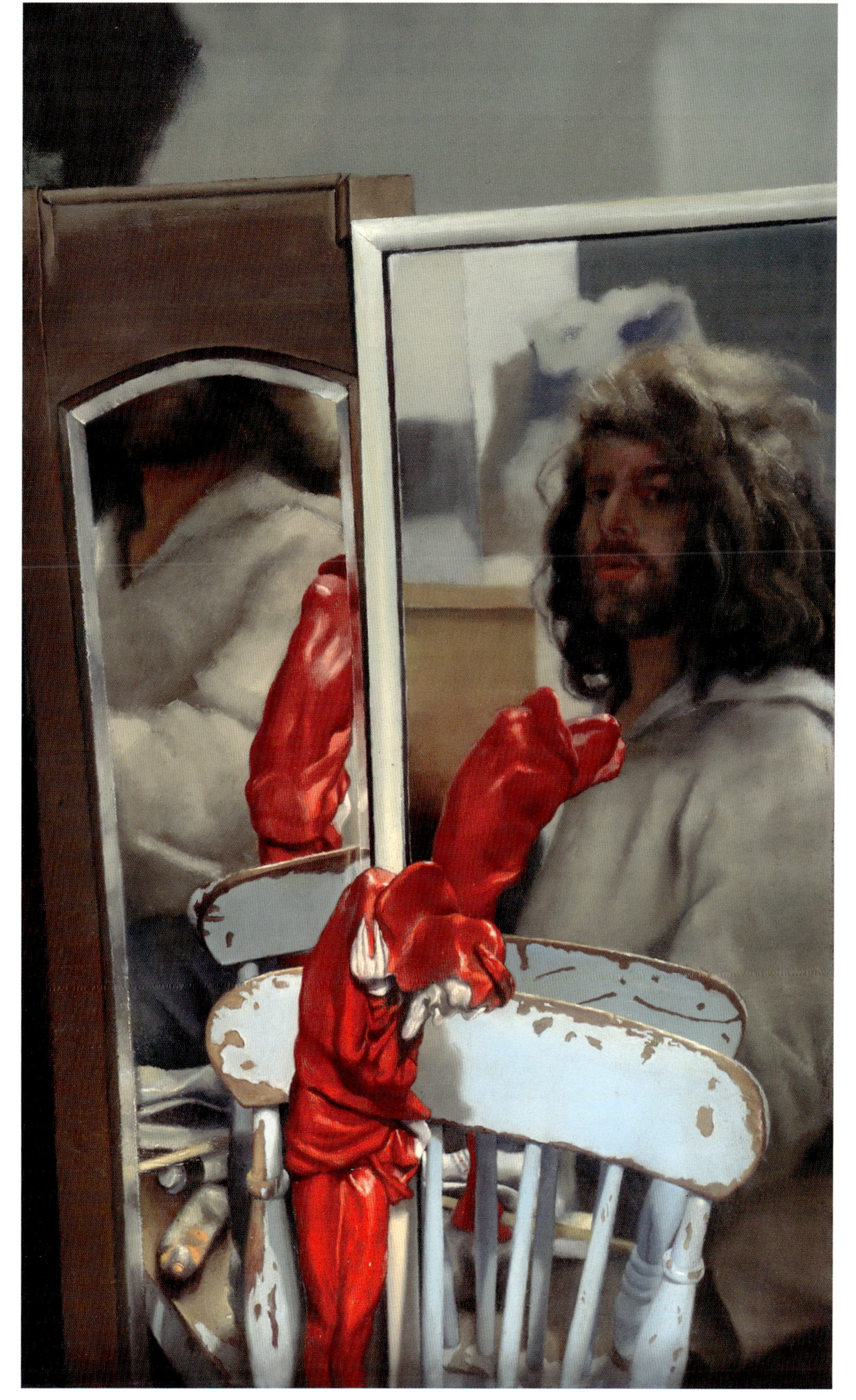

"I was aware that Rembrandt had produced some sixty self-portraits, that Van Gogh had produced a large number, and so on. But curiously I was most interested in the work of an obscure sculptor called Franz Xaver Messerschmidt, who had produced some seventy portraits of expressions. He believed that his body had been invaded by imps that were tormenting him in a particular kind of way. He was feeling some physical distress, and these physiognomies, for want of another word, are really quite extra-ordinary; with gaping, agonised expressions of one kind or another."

R.O. Lenkiewicz

1977
Self-Portrait.
Oil on canvas.
51 x 45 cm.

commentary or an inventory of a portrait remains powerless to penetrate the silence of the painted lips. Raphael, who no doubt is 'listening' to the discussion between Ptolemy and Zoroaster, is present, beside Sodoma, in *The School of Athens*. Filippino Lippi 'witnesses' St Peter's condemnation as Masaccio does his glory. Vasari, in the *Lives* of 1568, mentions eighty painters who are present in the frescoes or altarpieces they painted. These painters are present in their works even if their presence is like that of Dante – whom Virgil is guiding through hell – 'I know not, in truth, how I entered here…' Obstinately, ceaselessly, unrelentingly, we are dealing with a mirror. The mirror is misleading. It is a place of interrogation. Leonardo observes: 'A mirror with a flat surface contains a true painting at its surface.' To paint himself, the painter proceeds through this mirror. To portray oneself, to paint a portrait of oneself, to 'do' one's portrait, is to paint a mirror. And this mirror trails myths behind it. Alberti saw Narcissus as the inventor of painting. The painter is portraying himself. In front of his easel he is posing and painting. The canvas stands in front of him, stroke by stroke the look appears. He may refuse to see the 'object', he may see only the tone of the tone, the shape of the shape, the colour of the colour. But the look gradually emerges. This look scrutinises him, it confronts. To his left or his right is a mirror; he views a painter seated in a room used as a studio who is turning away from the canvas placed before him. A face remains, a look remains; he is aware that they are his own. He knows that they are those of a painter; but there they are, unaccompanied by any attribute. The look he examines stares at him. It is this look that accosts him: it is precise, incisive, relevant and immediate. Then the painter turns away towards the canvas on the easel. He is viewing the same features which, uncertain, roughed out, trait for trait, are those of the face he was examining a moment ago. The look is the same, a direct look, and now in the nearby mirror it turns away. He moves his paintbrush closer to the pupil of the eye watching him under the eye-lid that is yet only a line. He paints this look as he had just seen it in the mirror a moment ago.

The painter paints this look that summons him: he stares at it; he compels it to appear before him. This painted look is no vacant stare; it isn't the look of waiting that a pose held so often puts on a sitter's face. The look the painter is painting on the canvas is that of the painter in the act of looking; it is the look that only a few moments before was searching the mirror. On the easel the portrait is finished. The painter looks at the portrait, at the mirror; at the portrait, at the mirror, mirror and portrait are similar – the look and disposition of the face in each are alike. Then, maybe, this labour complete, the painter gets up and returns to its usual place the mirror he has taken the time to paint. The portrait remains, an authentic copy, a surrogate for the mirror now removed. The portrait is a record of the mirror; ephemeral and mobile, the reflection is frozen. The portrait looks at the painter. Painted in what was present time, the portrait watches the painter grow older, the portrait watches the face it once was become wrinkled with age. Indifferent, the portrait watches time, which from day to day discovers death.

The painter is dying.

The painter is dead.

The portrait alone remains, the last element of what was formerly this triangle in which the look, from reflection to reflection, from painter to mirror, from mirror to

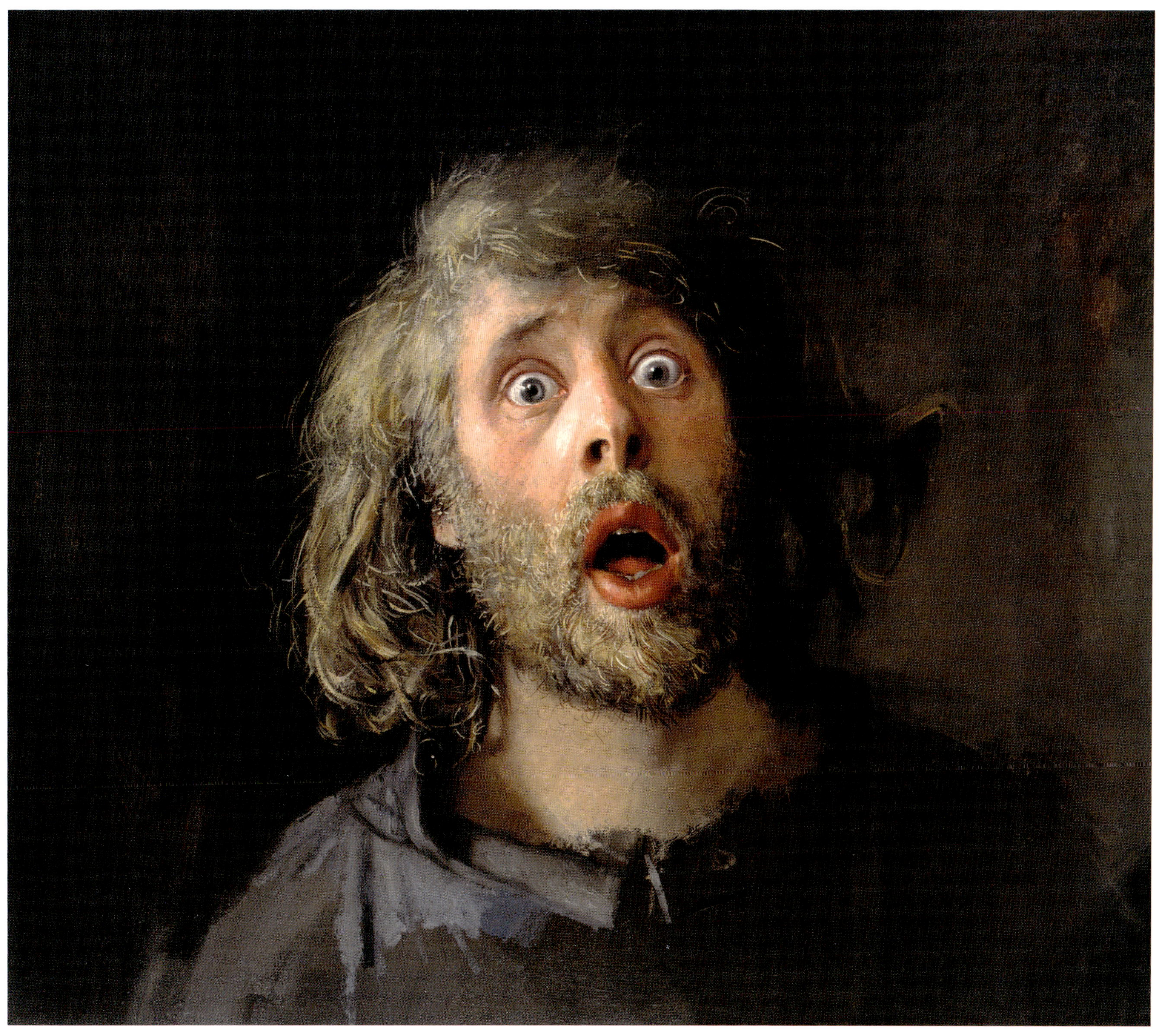

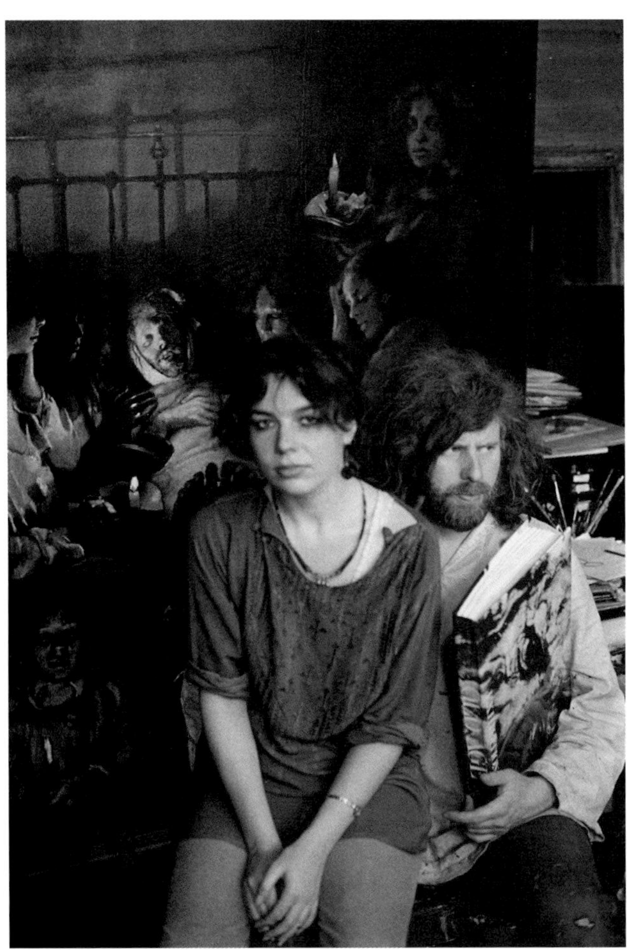

Eliza Massey with Robert, who is holding the *Old Age Project Notebook*, 1979. Three themes were developed that year – *Old Age, Suicide* and *Gossip on the Barbican*. The canvas *Self-Portrait on Death Bed* is seen behind. *Photo:* Dr P. Stokes.

painter, from painter to canvas, the look resolves and discovers itself commonplace, inasmuch as it belongs to three paths: the painter's, the mirror's, the canvas's.

I ('I' is the present reader) am looking at the canvas. I am looking at this other person whom I know to be a painter; I observe it. I consider its look, it catalogues me as I catalogue it. This look from 1496, 1639, 1787 or 1849, one month ago, yesterday, is present. I belong to a different period of time, and yet our eyes meet. We are one looking at each other squarely, standing face to face. The moment created by these looks cannot be placed within any chronology and acts as a delusion. What delusion is this 'other' time? The eyes watching are the eyes in a painted mirror in which I am looking at myself. Back and forth from like to like go the looks, but like differs from like and this to and fro is a delusion. The satisfaction and dissatisfaction of a gaze are but one. This is no longer Narcissus gazing at his reflection, but reflected eyes gazing at Narcissus. The painter paints himself, using a mirror. Speculum, mirror. Speculum, to speculate, speculation. Philosophers, thinkers and poets speculate. Studies, theories and theorems are speculations. Speculation defined the liberal Arts: Grammar, Arithmetic, Music, Geometry, Astronomy. The painter has no muse: neither Clio, nor Urania, nor Melpomene, nor Thalia, nor Terpsichore, nor Calliope, nor Erato, nor Polyhymnia, nor Euterpe had anything to do with painting. Mnemosyne, memory, their mother, forgot painting. The painter is a museless orphan who by eluding his specular portrait lays claim to a higher status.

R.O. Lenkiewicz
*Notes for an exhibition of studies from
Project 18 at the New Street Gallery, 1988*

1978
Self-Portrait.
Cryla on board.
40 x 28 cm.

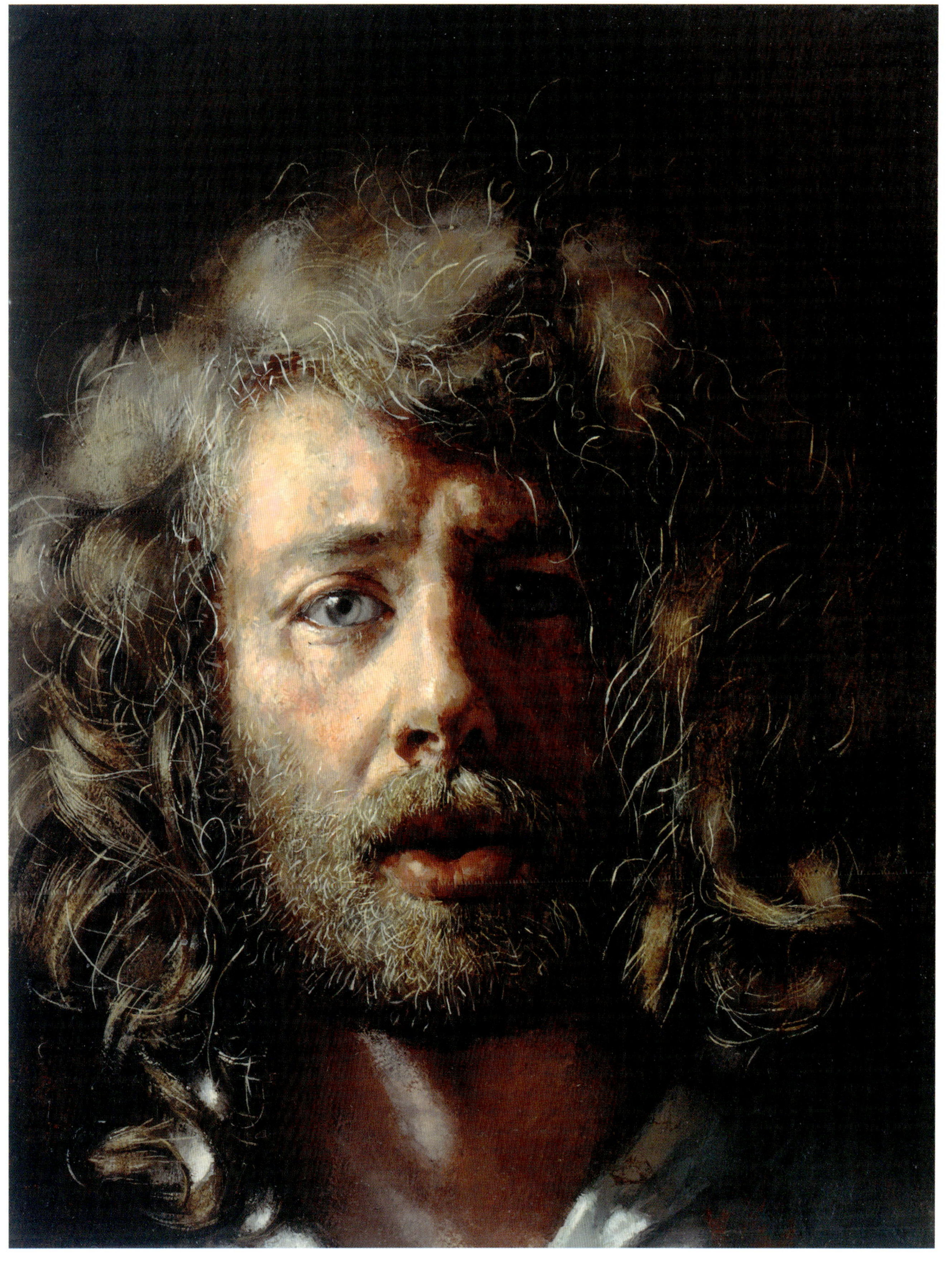

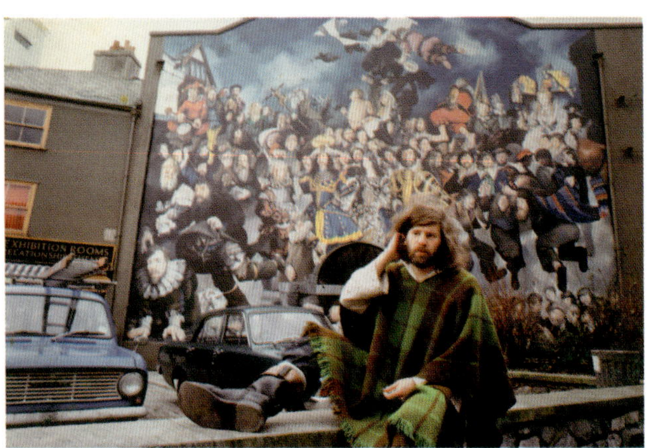

Robert Lenkiewicz seated in front of the *Barbican Mural* in 1979.
Photo: J.L. Bremer.

1979
Self-Portrait.
Oil on canvas.
75 x 62 cm.

'I don't see the business of family, generally speaking, as one of power and authority. I see it as one of suicide, one of self-negation, the consequence of terror and fear of isolation; that one creates a property group around one in order to sustain. No human being, in my view, wants to inflict himself upon and be inflicted upon by another human being for all of his life to the exclusion of all other people, more or less – even if that exclusion is highly ritualised.

In the case of the family, there is a procedure where one will achieve a level of psychosis for which one is willing to die. The family exists precisely because one does not wish to be creative. It is a means by which one can appear to render one's life significant, appear to give oneself overall responsibilities which are, I think, false responsibilities.

Some people would say: suicide is simply murder through mistaken identity. Now one could argue that the suicide *is* a kind of murderer, and indeed it might be murder on a massive scale. Look at it inversely – the suicide could be seen as somebody who by means of killing himself is obliterating the whole world. In actual fact, the suicide *is* annihilating the whole world: he is the greatest mass murderer that we know. To see the suicide as somebody who would be capable of megadeath on such a scale … it's an interesting idea, though probably stretched a bit, but generally speaking I see the suicide as somebody who finds his own or her own life, for one reason or another, intolerable and decides to put an end to it in the same way as he would put an end to anything that he found intolerable if he could. He can anthropomorphise that impulse in other ways, and one of the ways of doing that is to inflict upon oneself, and in most cases fairly ignorantly, a committed relationship to one human being to the exclusion relatively of all others.

It's a means by which one can control sexuality. It's a means by which, through the infliction of guilt and pseudo-responsibility, you can make sure that everything is in order; and I'm not sure that politics is anything other than an indirect consequence of that procedure. I've no more sympathy for politics than I have for the family: it's another means by which one abdicates. The average individual has had his sexuality so crushed, his own pleasure and joy, his own creative yes-saying to life, squashed so flat that the answer to a problem is a cross on a piece of paper, and let someone else deal with it? Of course, the more creative he was, the more he'd be willing and able to deal with his own situation – or, at any rate, meet people on those terms. And family is certainly a good means by which one can inflict this apathy and turn it, indirectly I suppose, into a political principle. That, for example, is one of the theses of Wilhelm Reich. In other ways, it's also a thesis of Nietzsche. But I'm sure in terms of my own aesthetic view that it's very applicable, though I think that more physiological knowledge is required.'

R.O. Lenkiewicz
Philip Stokes Notebooks, vol. 4, 4 Sep 1984

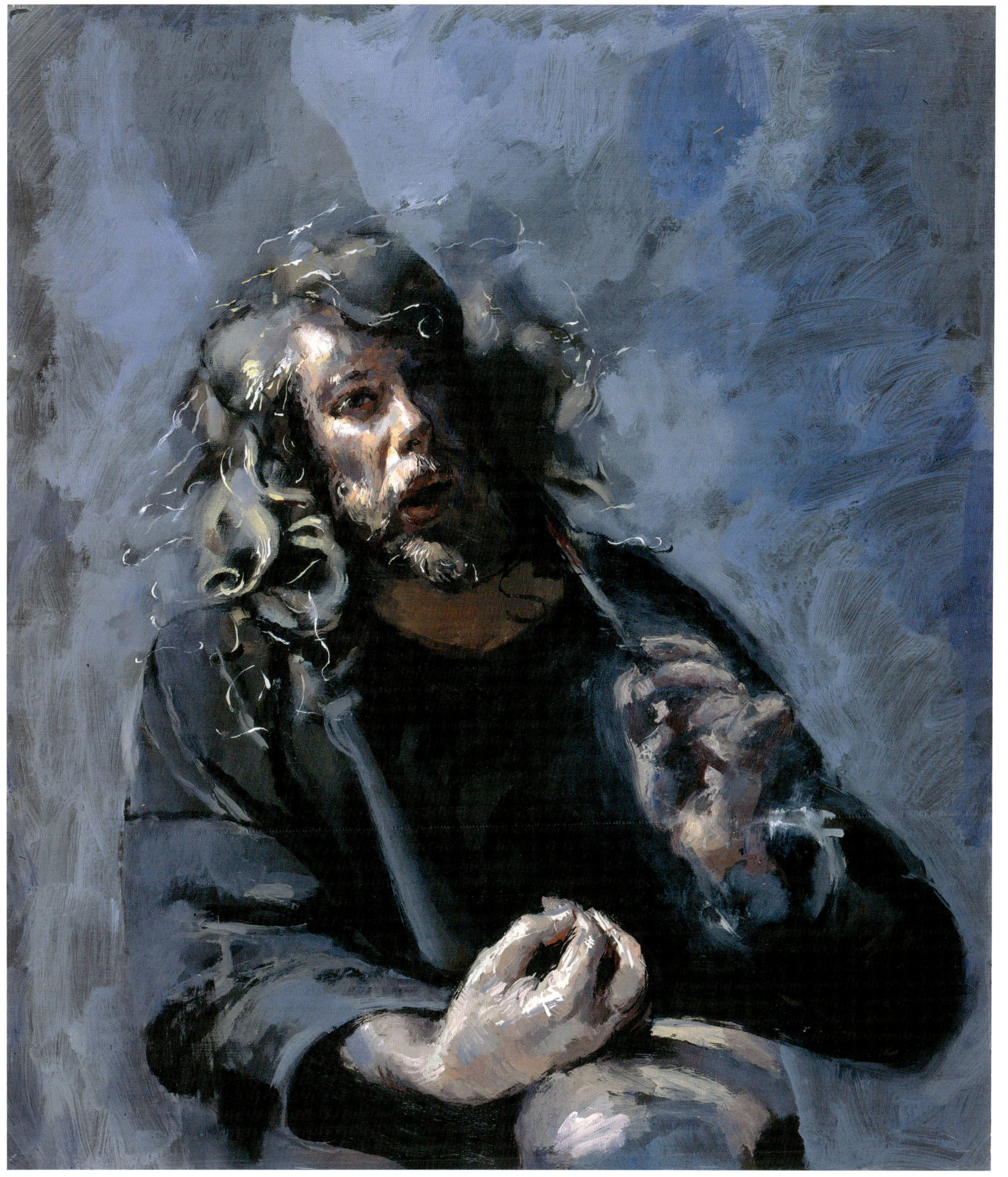

The original arrangement had been that we should meet at the Royal Academy, but the coincidence of the summer show with the Cézanne exhibition produced such crowds as to make this a doubtful tactic. I therefore rang Mary's address on the evening of the 26th and changed the venue to the British Museum.

Just before the appointed time I came out into the sun in the courtyard and looked around for Mary in the crowd. Eventually I settled down on the low wall near the entrance, and watched the people coming in. After a few minutes, I glanced behind me, and was surprised to see Mary walking down the steps of the Museum, thoroughly academic in spectacles and a cool blue cotton outfit which matched the day exactly.

I got out the red folder of photographs which she'd asked to see, and we went through them. I raised questions about the way Robert places himself so accurately against his paintings as to seem to be participating in them, and Mary agreed that this was so, remarking that Hockney does similarly. She mentioned that the white embroidered dress she appears in was one she'd bought herself – so that it's not as I thought it might be, part of the Lenkiewicz European family inheritance. A few identifications emerged for people in the photographs, of which the most interesting was of the woman lying under a tailor's male dummy in the Sexual Behaviour exhibition, who turned out to be Andrew Lanyon's wife. Mary remarked that the picture of Robert opening the alchemist's book and shaking his hair is unusual, since he is normally careful to assume a static pose.

When I began to ask about the circumstances of Mary's first meeting with Robert, I suggested that I switch on the tape recorder, but she did not entirely welcome this, and was mollified only by my offer to turn it off should she so wish. The following is a transcript of the bulk of our conversation, which dealt with Robert. The omissions concern digressions into art and photography, and other minor excursions.

Stokes. Anyway, you were saying that it was a very surreal sort of experience for you?

Mary.   Well yes, it was, when I first went. It was just so different from the conventional upbringing.

Stokes. What had you done, workwise or schoolwise? Were you already working away from home?

Mary.   No, I think I was probably still at school, but just leaving. I went into his studio with a friend of mine who was having a portrait done, and then he asked to see me; I was curious, and I went back.

Stokes. One of the contradictions which comes over to me, was when he said 'I never take responsibility for anybody.' Now that is a strange thing to say, because in many ways, from the outside, it looks as though he would have taken up certain responsibilities in your direction, and also of course for his

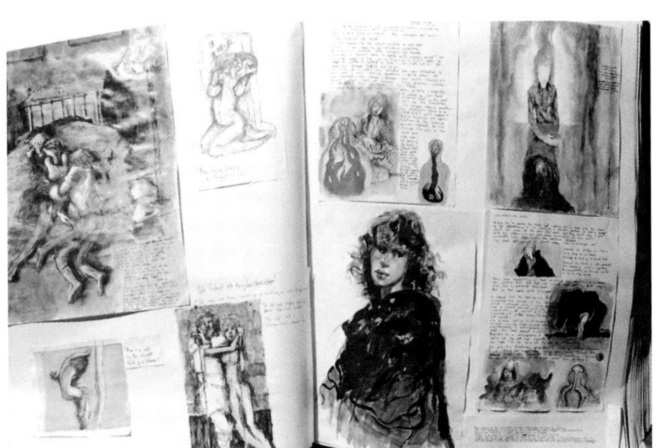

Mary: Aesthetic Notes 1978–1981. Elephant folio, 60 x 60 cm. The original volume in which all the aesthetic notes and journal entries relating to Robert's relationship with Mary were kept. *Photo*: Dr P. Stokes.

1980
Self-Portrait With Mary With Newspaper in Her Hair.
Oil on canvas.
127 x 127 cm.

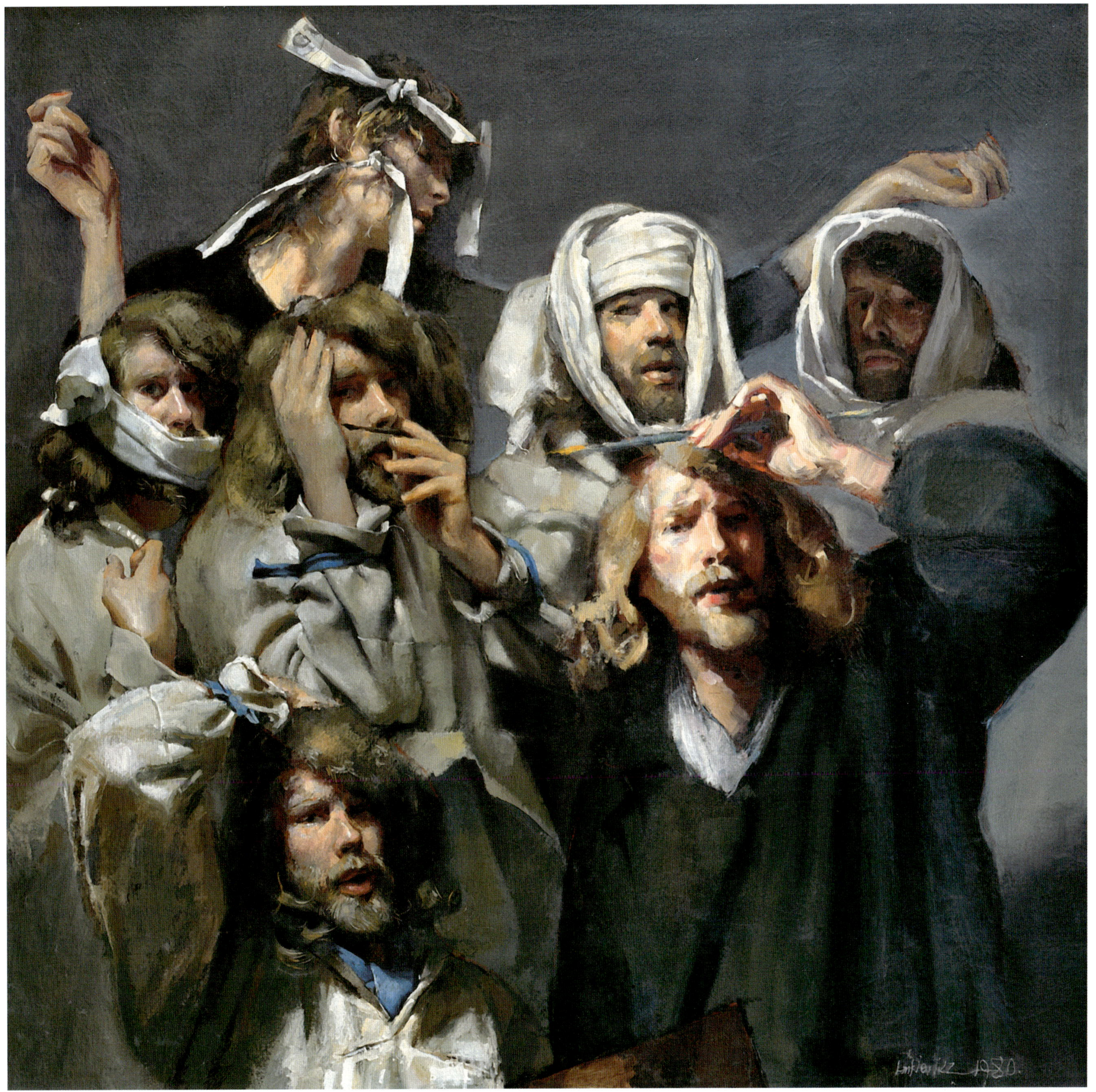

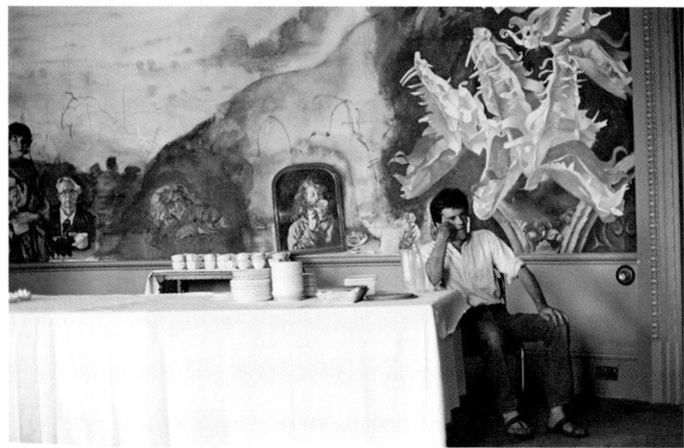

Peregrine, Lord Eliot, Robert's friend and patron seated in The Round Room at Port Eliot at the Elephant Fayre in 1983. *Photo*: Dr P. Stokes.

"There's a section which deals with the end of the world, The Deluge, that's inspired by Leonardo's extraordinary drawings of the Flood. It links with the Book of Job, *with* In Memoriam *by Tennyson, and also with the history of the Eliot family, and aspects of my life. It's a survey of nineteenth century attitudes towards the concept of tragedy, of the ending of things… A hotchpotch of enquiries, with a series of observations which constitute the riddle, which only one small part of the mural articulates and can only be seen in a reflection, in a particular kind of way."*

R.O. Lenkiewicz

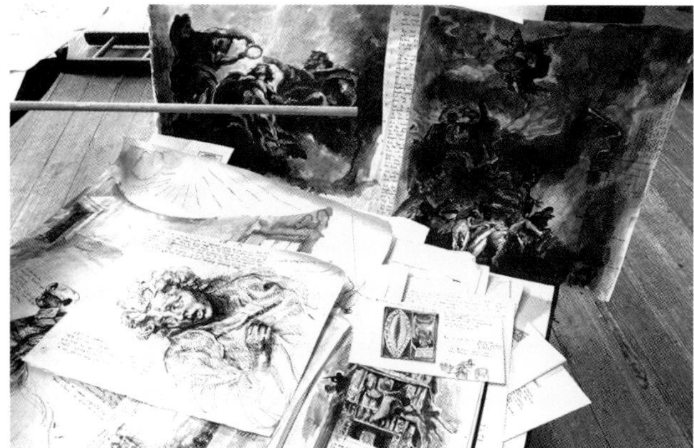

Preparatory sketches for *The Riddle Mural* in the 40 ft diameter Round Room at Port Eliot. *Photo*: Dr P. Stokes.

vagrants and for his Education Project, for all sorts of things and people who have benefited from, or have been involved with, Robert's abilities.

Mary.   He said the same thing to my father. He said that he didn't want and wouldn't take any responsibility for me or for his own children, and my father from that moment on disliked him, because he had sat there and said it to him directly. Once he has said that, it gives him the freedom of making the worst statement he possibly could, and then from that point he actually acts very differently. The nice thing from my point of view, when I entered into the relationship with him – I mean, I didn't realise when I first went that it was going to be a relationship – but when I first met him, because his reputation stood before him I wasn't blinded in any way. I knew the worst, first; and so what you uncover then is the secret side, outside the reputation.

Stokes. It ties up with the Nietzschean thing when again, I was talking about the ethical duty of the photographer to his subject, and he said, *'but an artist has no duty to the world except to know it'*. And at the same time, there's a contradiction there, because in knowing his vagrants, or Diogenes or whomever it is, he's actually involved himself in a way which is not morally neutral.

Mary.   Right, I think he definitely does. The relationships he has with people – obviously I'm just giving my point of view, because I was anxious and I didn't want to be used in any way – I was really worried about it. Over the years I've really watched the way he deals with people, and the way he deals with different types of relationships. And he's got different sets of relationships, and some of them are testing himself to see whether he just can. I think the one with me was that I was extremely shy, and very repressed, and very, very conventional, and it was a challenge for him to see whether he could get this one's interest. He enjoys a hunt, and also it feeds back into his painting, and he wants to feel it to its fullest extent; whether he does or not is another matter. I don't want to go too deeply into that.

Stokes. Robert does a lot of writing, doesn't he? He covers an enormous amount of ground with the books and the notes that he produces.

Mary.   I think his diaries are astounding. Actually, I was just thinking about what you were saying about whether he's manipulative or not. I think if you're worried about whether he's manipulative, then ninety per cent of the time he is because just everything he does is this combined artistic effort to express himself.

Stokes. I've always put it to myself as being a kind of universal theatre which occupies the whole of his life, and the whole of his environment.

Mary.   The thing is, that it is a theatre on the outside, but I think that he's so intense and sincere about it from his point of view, and he thinks that somehow, by noting all these things down, that there's going to be something positive about it, just by the sheer amount of information. Lord Eliot was saying to him at Easter that he was very foolish to leave his notebooks where he does leave them, because now and again one gets stolen and of course there are no copies. But he does diaries and he does aesthetic notebooks on particular relationships that he thinks are special in some way. And he does little paintings which are more expressive. If you think of the Kandinsky type of expression, he does that sort of thing, to evoke the atmosphere.

Stokes. 'He had a red feeling moving through his body …'

Mary. 'She had a pale blue aura round her left shoulder …'

Stokes. That's it. I've seen some of those in the work on you, haven't I?

Mary. Yes. He's done several of those. Every Project has got them in. What he puts in them is his very visual attempt to be quite academic about his studies, and full of information and sources. For every Project he reads as much information as he can, and so he either does paintings from the books, or mostly he records where he got the information from or things that are relevant to the painting or to his thought.

Stokes. It's a tremendous scholarly resource.

Mary. Yes, that's why he's so concerned that it's understood his work doesn't mean anything in one isolated painting. He's concerned to have a whole Project.

Stokes. Peregrine, I suppose, is one of Robert's patrons, isn't he? In respect of *The Round Room Mural* at least?

Mary. Yes, Robert's spent so long painting it, that he quite enjoys going down and Perry quite likes his company, and I think there's some peculiar arrangement about the rent of the studio.

Stokes. Is the project on the house in Priory Road taking off?

Mary. I was absolutely astounded when I went to visit Myriam, who's living there at the moment, at Easter. The whole of the upstairs is turned into a large barn and its atmosphere is completely changed. One of the major conflicts between Robert and myself was that I love the sun, and he likes [laughs] the opposite.

Stokes. The School of Dark Things!

Mary. Yes, and so we always had these fights over the windows [laughs], and so in the house he's changed the atmosphere completely. It was just so horrible and frightening and enclosed before.

Stokes. Only that one window on the landing open.

Mary. And now Robert's opened up the windows, and made it this wonderful style of wooden blocks … and he was telling me how it's related to when we went to Italy years ago, and we were sitting in those cloisters and noticing the wonderful atmosphere … there's no doubt about the fact that it's changed from this room of horror. It's still magical, but it's magical in a much more positive sense.

Stokes. It did seem to me to be almost forcedly dark when I went there.

Mary. It's lovely now. You've got a wonderful view right across the valley.

Stokes. Robert said, whether it was for effect or not, that he was going to obtain a few corpses and store them under the library.

Mary. There's a complete and utter mess, a whole rubbish tip underneath. There's the hole in the ground that he decided to build when he was extending downwards.

Stokes. Has he got the two premises together yet?

Mary. I think it's bought, because he mentioned bank arrangements. The only time I've ever seen Robert embarrassed – this goes back to his idea of responsibility – is when the only way that he could get a mortgage was to do it through my bank account. I've still got one bank account which is Lenkiewicz, and I would never have anything to do with finances with him, because he's always in such a mess. He had an overdraft about ten years ago and the bank wouldn't let him have a new bank account, and so he had to ask me to put it through my account.

Stokes. I've had the Education Project books hard bound, and they look very well. It's going to be a very good source of material, but it probably needs indexing, which I don't think I've got the time to do; but it's fascinating to read.

Mary. In a way it reminds me slightly of the Shere Hite *Reports*, the style he's chosen to adopt – quite a good way to document something. Nobody would actually sit there and read through the whole thing, but you could; it's all collected there together and ready for somebody to analyse. The evidence is there.

Stokes. Do you feel that you've induced any changes of view? Partnered any particular developments between you?

Mary. In Robert? No, except that he wasn't allowed to do anything bad to me. So I had to represent his good side [laughs], otherwise I would have just left. So that's what he says. I don't know; I think he's *thoroughly* bad really!

Stokes. Yes, probably.

Mary. Mm. That's difficult to say, really.

Stokes. You're not stood back from it, are you? You were involved, so you can't tell.

Mary. I'm very distant from him now, but I still feel extremely strongly in a particular way. Maybe it's the way we think. I learned an awful lot about his paintings, and about him, so I still feel really close.

Stokes. Were you concerned with art before? Or is that something which came out of this association?

Mary. No, I quite enjoyed making craft. In fact I was thinking back to what you were saying before … one of the major things I was curious about was the whole artistic world that I hadn't experienced.

Stokes. And the initiation into it?

Mary.   And ideas; just everything. There's more than the 'theatre' of it: it was this whole idea of lots of new things [inaudible]. I only understood about one in every five words that he said, which made me frustrated, made me want to know more. And the thing generated. It also caused me a lot of angst, [laughs] but you either become positive, and learn more, or …

Stokes. Do you think he'll go on doing the *Relationship Series*, or is he going to turn round and say, now that's it, I shall go and do something totally different? He thought of studying medicine at one time, didn't he?

Mary.   I can't see him doing anything different, because basically he can't really exist outside his studio without knocking people down and generally being socially unacceptable [laughs].

Stokes. It was interesting to see when we called into Karen's house, how very much like an extension of the Robert territory that is. She sat with very much of a sense of theatre under the light at the opening, didn't she? I had a lovely set of photographs there, or enough photographs came out to be lovely, anyway.

Mary.   I'm sure that there's a theatre that's set up when people are around. But I don't know if you've noticed, that it's deflecting away from his paintings, and it's like a cover-up for them. And when he's talking to the people that he's painting, he's very rarely talking about his paintings.

Stokes. It's interesting how you get this compartmentalisation; how you get one lot of visitors and another lot, and they're kept very separate. There might be oneself there, and somebody will call in and he'll go and talk to them and somebody else will appear and be kept in a third place, and Robert will do the rounds between them, like that.

Mary.   In nearly everything, nearly every part of his very varied life, the thing that means the most to him is the painting; that's the thing he doesn't really communicate to other people very much. And it's because that's what he's most sensitive about, that's what he wants to keep totally … pure if you like. A kind of very innocent representation.

1981
The Painter With Mary in Newspaper
Magi-Fools Hats.
Oil on canvas.
48 x 69 cm.

Stokes. A marvellous raconteur, isn't he? And so is John. For someone in the therapeutic world, he produces stories with the most incredible Freudian or psychoanalytic connotations; which he either recognises and incorporates as part of the game, or one simply finds they are so natural that he hasn't even thought of the connotations. He's talked about the family, and there's the most amazing narratives about little minor events, like you might have in a dream, with these strange connotations to them.

Mary.   It could be something he's thinking about that he's turned into a story.

Stokes. Yes, it was marvellous. Incredible!

Mary.   With Robert, sometimes it's just that someone has come in and told him the latest Beano story, and that's triggered off a whole lot of associations for him. So I think he flits in and out of being serious, but it's a very Jewish way to flit in and out of being serious, and turn it into humour, and then contrasting it back to something serious again.

Stokes. Have you ever got to the bottom of the Baron Schlossberg thing?

Mary.   No. Don't know what all that is about [laughs].

Stokes. I've got contacts in Munich and thereabouts, and I've had them looking out. There is a Barony of Schlossberg in Bavaria, but it's an old one. Nobody can trace a new creation by King Ludwig II, and nobody who I managed to get in touch with, and I think I've been fairly lucky with that, has actually located a Schlossberg-ascribed piece of work in Neue Schwanstein.

Mary.   When he did it, he wouldn't have been Schlossberg, would he?

Stokes. No, he wouldn't. That's the point – he'd have been called something else. I'll have to go there one day.

Mary.   I'd like to go.

Stokes. Yes. What shall you do when you've finished at the university?

Mary.   Ah, well, I'm afraid I don't know [laughs].

Stokes. I wondered if you were working some grand plan?

Mary.   My grand plan was getting here, you see, and I suddenly realised that after about ten years of struggle I'm almost at the end of it; I don't know what to do now. I just feel totally incompetent all the way round.

Stokes. You'll probably live by teaching for the OU for a bit, or something like that.

Mary.   I think things tend to happen to me.

Stokes. If you remain receptive, they do don't they? I would say the same.

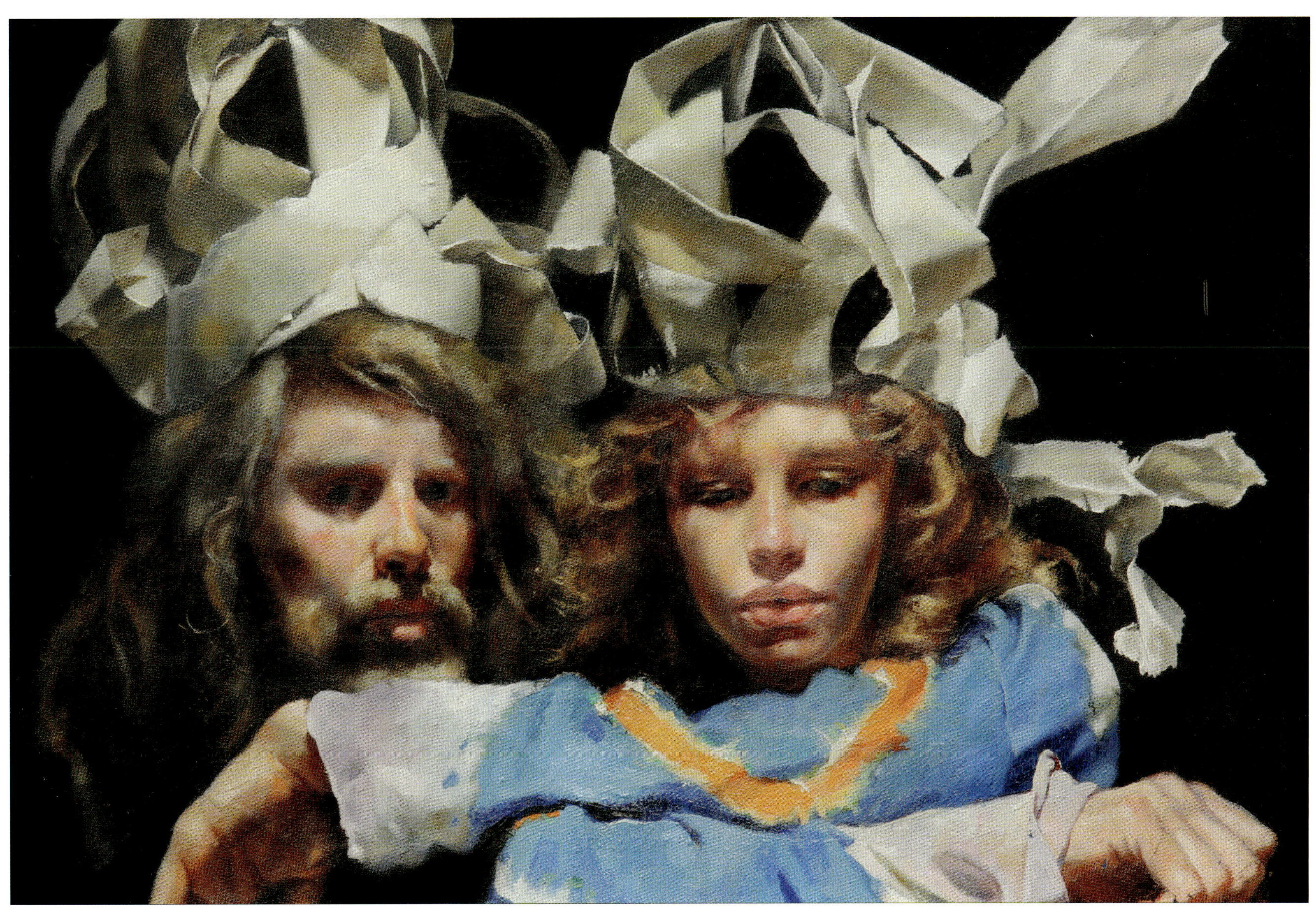

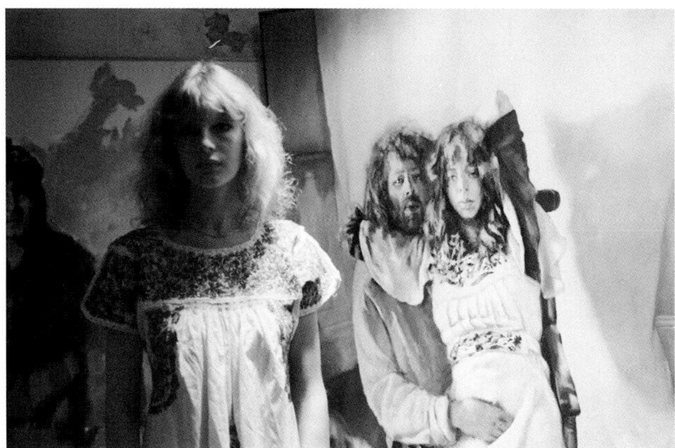

Mary at Robert's home in Compton in 1982 standing in front of the canvas *Self-Portrait with Eliza* from the *Self-Portrait Project*. *Photo*: Dr P. Stokes.

"Robert sometimes said of himself 'I can be seen from certain points of view as a Dr Mengele figure' and would be somewhat amoral, by which I mean he would have no regard for the impact of his, if you'll excuse the phrase, 'penetrating research' on the women he related to.

Of course, he would also apply that procedure to himself; for example, with Mary. He had very strong feelings for Mary and he observed himself having those feelings. She eventually left – good for her – and he observed his feelings during that process too."

John Lenkiewicz, 2008

Stokes. How many children's Robert got? I saw such a lot at the opening of the exhibition that I couldn't count them.

Mary. I'm not sure that I can count them anymore, either!

Stokes. He did say years ago that he'd got twelve, but that was probably rhetorical and so long ago.

Mary. I think it must be ... there weren't twelve, there might be a few mysterious extras ... and then there's a new daughter ...

Stokes. One died, or was impaired in some way.

Mary. Yes, that one died. But that was rather a nasty experience for him, I think.

Stokes. I gathered that. He mentioned it to me. But at the time he mentioned it, he was clearly upset, and I didn't pursue it.

Mary. Yes, he was. I'm sure he was.

Stokes. He was trying to be urbane, but underneath you could tell he wasn't.

Mary. But this is again the lack of responsibility thing. Some of them are definitely part of relationships and very close.

Stokes. In many ways Robert's family seems very close to him – they come in and talk and are instructed and exchange views, all that sort of thing.

Mary. This is the contradiction in him saying that he's not responsible. What he means by that is more that you should feel, whether you can do it not, that any other children should be just as close to you. That brings up a lot of problems, like the fact that you can only identify with a certain number. I suppose after that, you can't have that sort of closeness with the whole world.

Stokes. I suppose that's like in my own family, only one of them is my actual child, but it's as though they all were.

Mary. All Karen's children, I mean the two eldest, aren't his children, but he's extremely close to those children and he treats them as though they're his, and I've seen him behave with other people's children in the same way. There's an enormous range of ages, as well, among the children.

Stokes. There must be some in their twenties, mustn't there?

Mary. Yes, the oldest one is called Dorian, and he's a bit older than Alice. Alice is the next eldest; she's Mouse's daughter and Robert married Mouse when she was pregnant. I think it was while he was at the Royal Academy, but I don't know.

Stokes. When I first met Robert in 1968 – which was a strange meeting anyway – there was a new baby there then, and he'd got drawings of it being born, on the wall.

Mary. That might have been Annie's child, Kate.

Stokes. What about the esoteric philosophies, Rosicrucianism, the occult, that sort of thing?

Mary. He's got a big collection of books on those kinds of subjects, but I think he's very careful when people come to get information from him when they find out that he's got a collection of alchemical or occult works. He stays very objective about all religions and he doesn't get emotionally involved in any of it.

Stokes. I've noticed that. I'm very interested because I assume that he's a very strong Jewish background which would have a high level of commitment, at his root anyway. Maybe he's evolved from that point, and changed a little.

Mary.   Apart from the fact that he would say 'there's no anti-Semite like a Jewish anti-Semite'; that's one of his favourite sayings. He's interested in cross-linking different cultures and different forms of religion and alchemy; fascinations of that kind that try to explain the unexplainable, and draw attention to it.

Stokes. We talked briefly once on that in a very, very noisy café. It was an interesting conversation, but such a clatter going on that it couldn't really take off.

Mary.   You just have to take one look round his library to see what he's interested in. He's got certain favourite books. We sometimes do this tour of the library; in fact we always do this tour of the library – it's really funny! When I come home I have to see the most recent book, or I have to touch the special books of the library, and then put them back again with due celebrity.

Stokes. Well, this has been a fantastic conversation.

Mary.   I don't know whether I've managed to explain things well enough ...

Stokes. I think you have.

Mary.   But I suppose it's quite a personal ... I mean there's ten years of on and off contact. I go through phases of missing quite a lot, but it's a bit like having a very strong foundation because I was just with him 24 hours a day for several years, and then you can kind of break off, knowing that what's going on at the root isn't going to be all that different. One of the nice things of having such a separate existence is that when I go back a) I can test whether there's still a bond there or not, and b) it's nice to see how things have changed.

Stokes. I approve of separate existences, I think.

Mary.   It's quite nice to have that book at the back of your head that's linked to somebody's at the back of their heads somewhere else [laughs].

END

When I had turned the recorder off, Mary began to talk about the more feminist issues of modelling for Robert, and otherwise taking part in his events. About, for instance, the way in the first television film (not *The Leaves Were Full of Children*, since I haven't seen it) she had been included as the silent 'pretty lady', a role of which she no longer approved. About the way in which Robert uses a model either as a wholly determined and controlled element in his compositions; or else interactively in the sense of setting up a situation to which Mary, or whoever, is to react and be observed in the process. I couldn't see that this was either a novel revelation, or an unusual indictment of Robert as an artist, but Mary clearly feels she might be construed as disloyal or otherwise hurtful if recorded as saying so, and left a scatter of semi-retractions and conditional clauses lying around at the end of it all.

My conclusion was that Mary's discretion, even reticence, partly derived from her upbringing and partly from her longstanding loyalty to Robert, is as strong as it's ever been. In the light of what must have been, in every sense, the opening experience of living with Robert, this is a tribute to the fundamental strength of Mary's character; and, very likely, to the limitations of Robert's abnegation of his responsibility towards her. Nevertheless, given Mary's undoubted intelligence, I'm a little surprised that after the successful academic period, she is still unconfident and uncertain of direction for the future, almost as might be a confused sixth former. I therefore wonder if, despite a feminist awareness that I guess Mary can articulate pretty effectively when she needs it, she is still at heart or in part the 'pretty lady' she affects to despise, that in certain ways Mary might indeed be a latter-day analogy of a Pre-Raphaelite woman?

I hope we shall speak again some day.

Page 18 of *The Mary Notebook* dated 24 February 1978.

1981
Self-Portrait Fantasising Playing Mary Like a Cello.
Oil on sailcloth.
51 x 43 cm.

'It seemed as though the skull was surrounded by my "red" – fed from across the table and that her cold wilting form was vanishing like a ghost by its merciless presence. The photograph of myself as a child still making a whitish line to her eye. The yellow surround seemed to disappear to her left as she slid down into air. No sexual feelings – but captivated by her blue-greyness. Sense of loss as I saw her off at the Co-op staircase. Addictive state serious.'

R.O. Lenkiewicz
From Page 18 of The Mary Notebook

'[The aesthetic notes] are to be understood as illustrations of an aesthetic theory about human relationships. They have no direct link to his large-scale Projects and other paintings; or to any theses about 'art'.

Over the last 25 years Lenkiewicz has studied his own relationships in ruthless detail. A large book (sometimes involving the help of the partner) is begun as the relationship commences, and the book is maintained throughout the duration of the relationship. Several hundred of these books (richly illustrated) testify to the general observation that the assumption of concern and regard for our partners has little to do with their welfare. Obsessional and addictive attitudes are cross-referential in our lives; art, men/women/children, ideologies, all are subject to purely aesthetic and physiological responses. The belief that we are concerned for the welfare of another person – independently of our own needs – is of a pathological character.

The alcoholic, the heroin addict, the artist, the lover, the business man, the theologically and the politically committed, all show the same addictive pathways. In responding preferentially in our lives (companions, environments, beliefs), we are rendering ourselves victim to physiological addictions of an entirely aesthetic nature. The failure to recognise with an "unsentimental humanity" our isolation in the scheme of things, brings about the lurid, brutal and sometimes cruel assumption that our "attraction" to things, people and ideas might mean that we "love" them. For "love" to make sense we would have to be non-selective and aesthetically dead; in the light of our as yet limited knowledge of human physiology, this would be an irrational expectation.

We are profoundly insensitive to our own aesthetic vulnerability, and studying this procedure can be salutary and humanising.'

R.O. Lenkiewicz
Notes for an exhibition of Aesthetic Notes
at the New Street Gallery, 1987

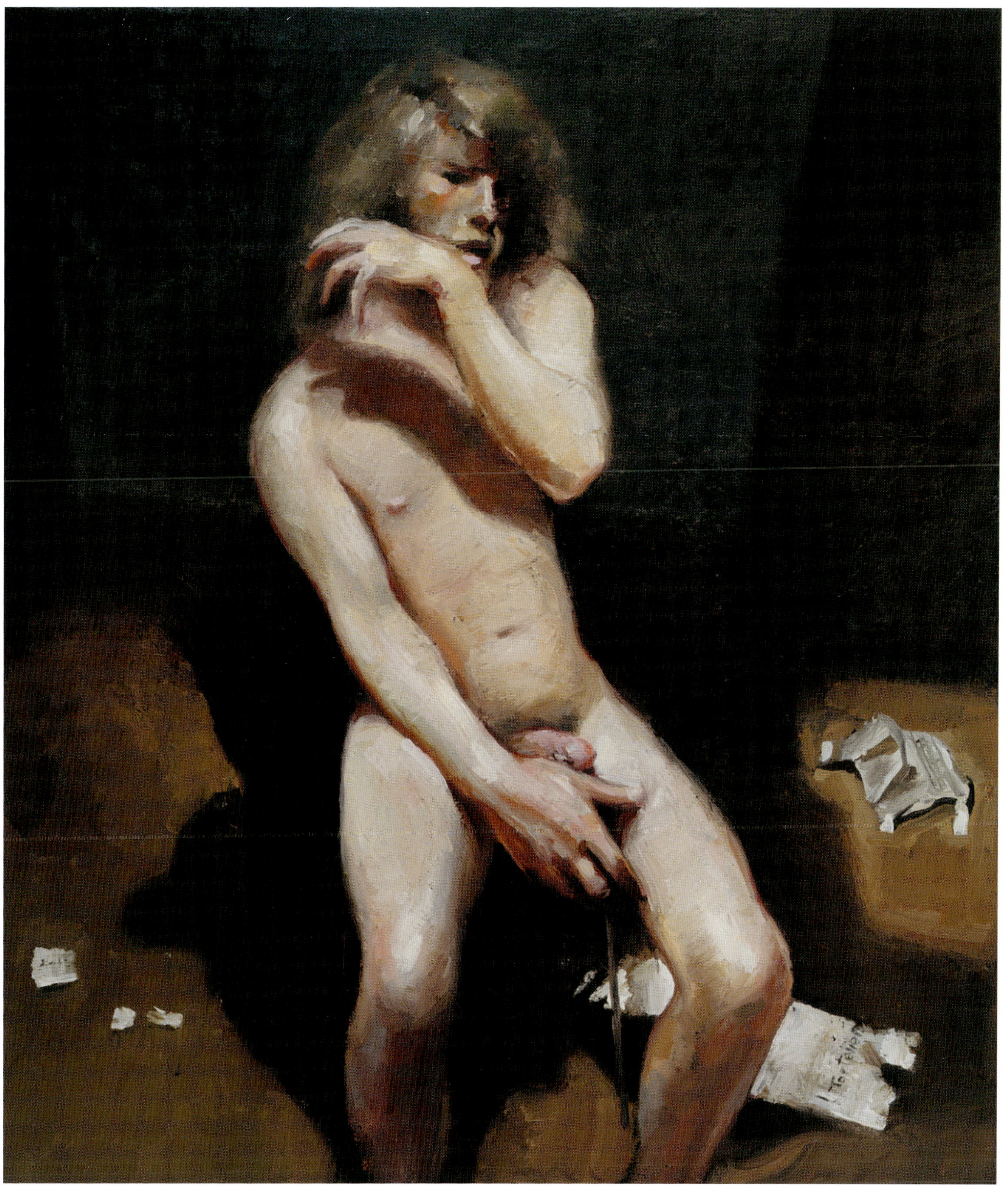

'If you know of anyone who is dying maturely and would be willing to pose for a painting please leave information at these studios.'

Notice posted in the window of The Barbican Studio in 1981

'After so many centuries of death familiarity and confrontation, and in such fascinating and tireless variation, we are now witness and contributors to an extraordinary event. Death is being effaced, disappearing.

Death is shameful and forbidden. It began surreptitiously enough: those surrounding the dying person had a tendency to 'spare' him, to hide from him the 'gravity' of his condition. The truth was being interfered with. But this sentiment (highly suspect in itself) was rapidly replaced by an urgent need to avoid – no longer for the sake of the dying person, but for society's sake, for the sake of those close to the dying person – the fact of death; the ugliness of death.

From 1930 onwards one no longer died at home, in the family environment, but in the hospital – alone. Once the hospital had been a shelter for the poor, for pilgrims: it became a centre for healing. It still has a curative function, but it is also a designated spot for dying. One goes to the hospital for the specific purpose of dying. More than 70% of people die in hospital, three quarters of them alone. Death has become a technical phenomenon obtained by the cessation of care determined by a doctor and hospital team. The dying person has probably lost consciousness, his death has been cut into little segments: 'heart death', 'brain death', 'cellular death' and so on.

In the 19th century a sentimental pattern caused the initiative to pass from the dying man to his family. Today the initiative has passed from the family (as much an outsider as the dying person) to the hospital team. They are the masters of death. It is they who obtain from their patient an 'acceptable' death; that is, a death that can be tolerated by the survivors. Too much sorrow no longer inspires sympathy but repugnance – a sign of instability or bad manners. You may cry if no one sees or hears it.

Where mourning is repressed the mortality rate of widows or widowers during the following year rises. A single person is missing for you and the whole world is empty. But one no longer has the right to say so aloud. Meaningful participation in the process of dying removes much of the despair of the survivors.'

R.O. Lenkiewicz
From The Changing Pattern of Dying,
Western Evening Herald, 11 Feb 1982

1978
Self-Portrait – Three Stages (After Titian).
Oil on board.
61 x 51 cm.

1982
The Painter Holding Himself When Ninety.
Emulsion on canvas.
145 x 99 cm.

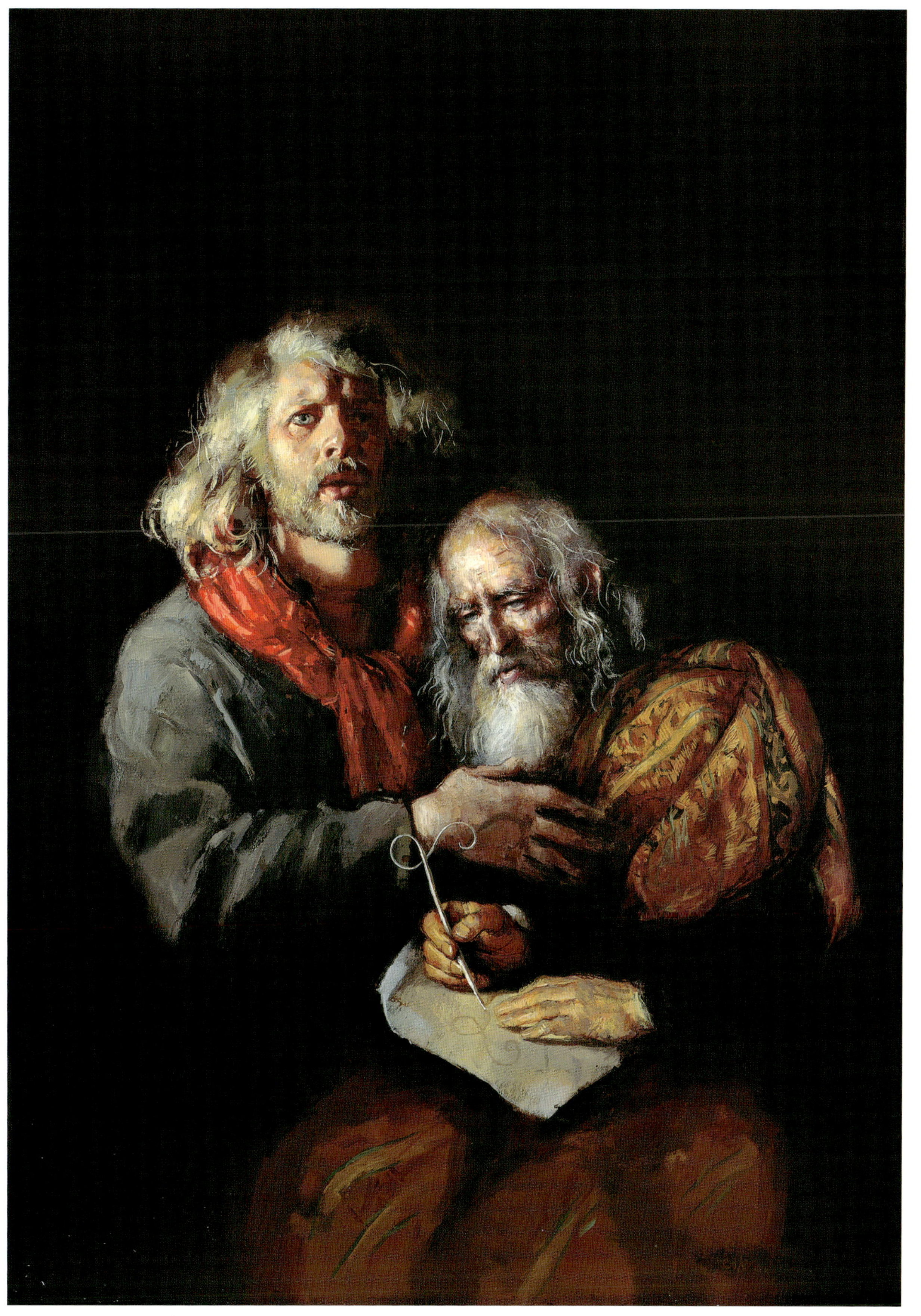

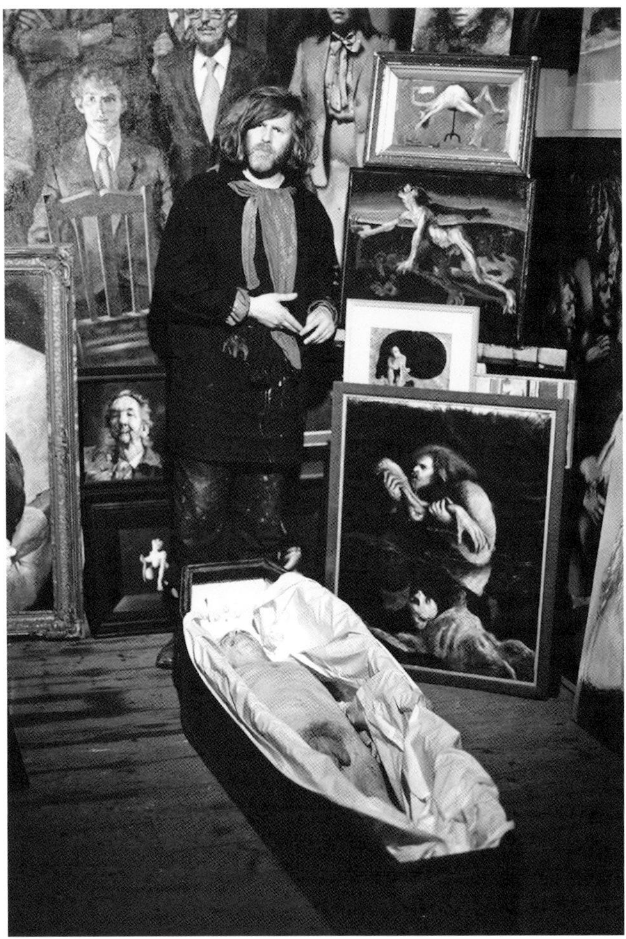

The ultimate memento mori: Robert Lenkiewicz with the embalmed body of the vagrant Edwin MacKenzie, or Diogenes, in 1985. *Photo*: Dr P. Stokes.

'In many ways the death of children is the least easy thing to understand, particularly for a believer. Yet believers have a precedent because God, in a sense, is a child murderer … He lives in a Byronic style up in Heaven; creating, creating, creating. But he's so inconceivably lonely – as he's all *aeternitatis*, he can't die, rather like the Wandering Jew. And so he cuts himself in half by having a son: then kills him. So there's a precedent for a child murderer up in Heaven.'

R.O. Lenkiewicz
Philip Stokes Notebooks, vol. 2, 1987

'Perhaps the most startling of the *Black Paintings* was inspired by the picture *Saturn Devouring His Son* painted in 1636 by Rubens. Goya must have seen this painting in the Royal collection in Madrid. Rubens's god is set in the middle of the composition. The anatomy is idealised, the horror of the scene underplayed. The god's face is averted as he is caught up by the task in hand; the only legible expression is the child's anguished face. Goya transforms this baroque model.

His giant is literally off balance, leaning in from the side of the composition, as if unexpectedly caught in our view. His anatomy emerges piecemeal from the darkness; sinewy, aged, no idealisation. The child being eaten is beyond reaction. The focus is shifted to the crazed expression of the god, an embodiment of paranoia and fear.

Early Victorian photographs of this painting indicate that the god's sadistic ravings were graphically represented by an erect phallus – removed before the paintings were put on public view. Apparently the detail of a bloody, half-eaten corpse was less offensive to nineteenth century taste.

What do these paintings mean? We must remember the 'positioning' of each of the fourteen or so paintings on the two floors. Goya's *Saturn* was on the ground floor. Saturn, god of melancholy and time, an emblem of the ageing artist's own pessimism, was seen to dominate the scene.'

R.O. Lenkiewicz
Remarks on Goya at Plymouth Arts Centre
before a screening of Goya In Bordeaux, *1999*

1982

The Father Eats His Son.

Cryla on paper laid on board.

84 x 66 cm.

Monica: *Vagrancy*, *Mental Handicap* and *Old Age* were the greatest exhibitions. People used to wonder why he pretended in 1981 that he had died (when he was hiding at Perry's) and Robert came up with all sorts of reasons why. But those weren't the real reasons; I know because we discussed it in detail. He worked so, so hard on the *Old Age* theme [1979] and they were such beautiful paintings, and sod all people came to look at them. It was a beautiful exhibition and I remember him being so frustrated … he said 'People will only be interested in the work when I am dead.'

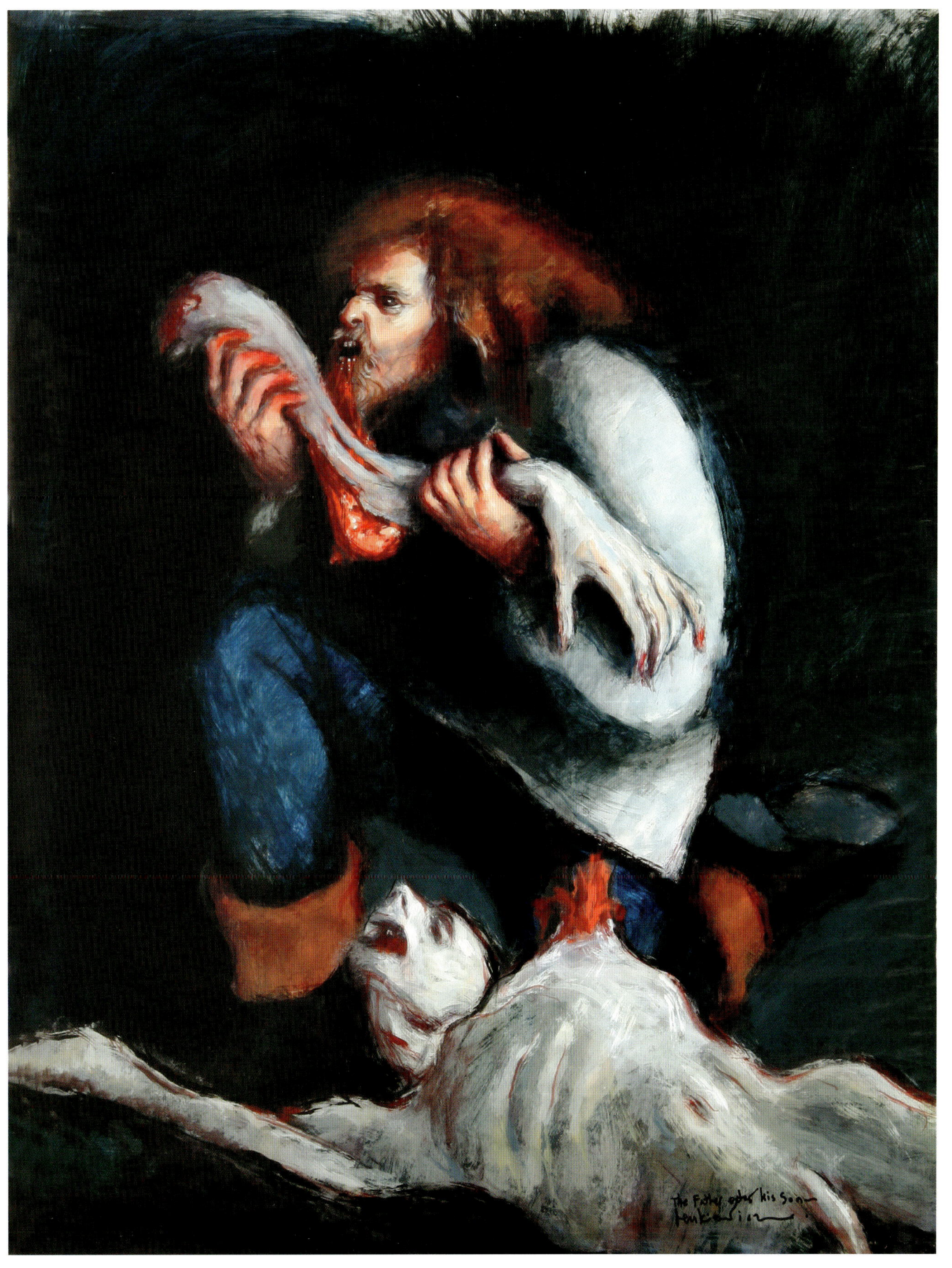
The Father and his Son

The Deposition – The Burial of Education diptych, centrepiece of
the *Observations on Local Education Project*, seen at the Barbican
Studio. *Photo*: D. Burd.

The present collection articulates the suggestion that slavery did not fade away with
Wilberforce and Lincoln; rather, it has continued into present day education.
It has found a level of social acceptability (primarily commercial), that has become
so strong that we regard it now as one of our greatest achievements.
The education for work policy has in recent years been fuelled with a sense of
urgency even panic, the brutalising effect of which presents further evidence of the
horror and the terror with which the adult views the child.

We witness at present and for some time to come the startling and dominant feature
of contemporary education throughout the Western world; the hatred felt by the adult
for the child.

R.O. Lenkiewicz
Studio, Barbican
Plymouth

THE DEPOSITION

This piece is related to Mahler's cycle of five orchestral songs; *Songs on the Deaths
Of Children* (Kindertotenlieder). The last song in particular, with lines such as, 'But
out of the house they've borne them. I had no say in the matter!', expresses quite
unforgettably the grief over the most incomprehensible of deaths. The mass
commercialising of the young, with its ensuing brutalised sensitivities, now operate
so collectively and with such grand-scale obeisance, that in the far future we may
reflect upon present day educational policy with the discomfort normally allocated for
the Holocaust. A book of notes and graphics runs parallel with this painting; these
notes are not in the present exhibition.

R.O. Lenkiewicz
Exhibition Notes to a showing of the Education Project *during the
1987 Cambridge Festival, sponsored by Lenkiewicz patron Sam Alper*

1988
The Deposition – The Burial of Education.
(Detail).
Oil on canvas.
350 x 280 cm (vertical panel of diptych).

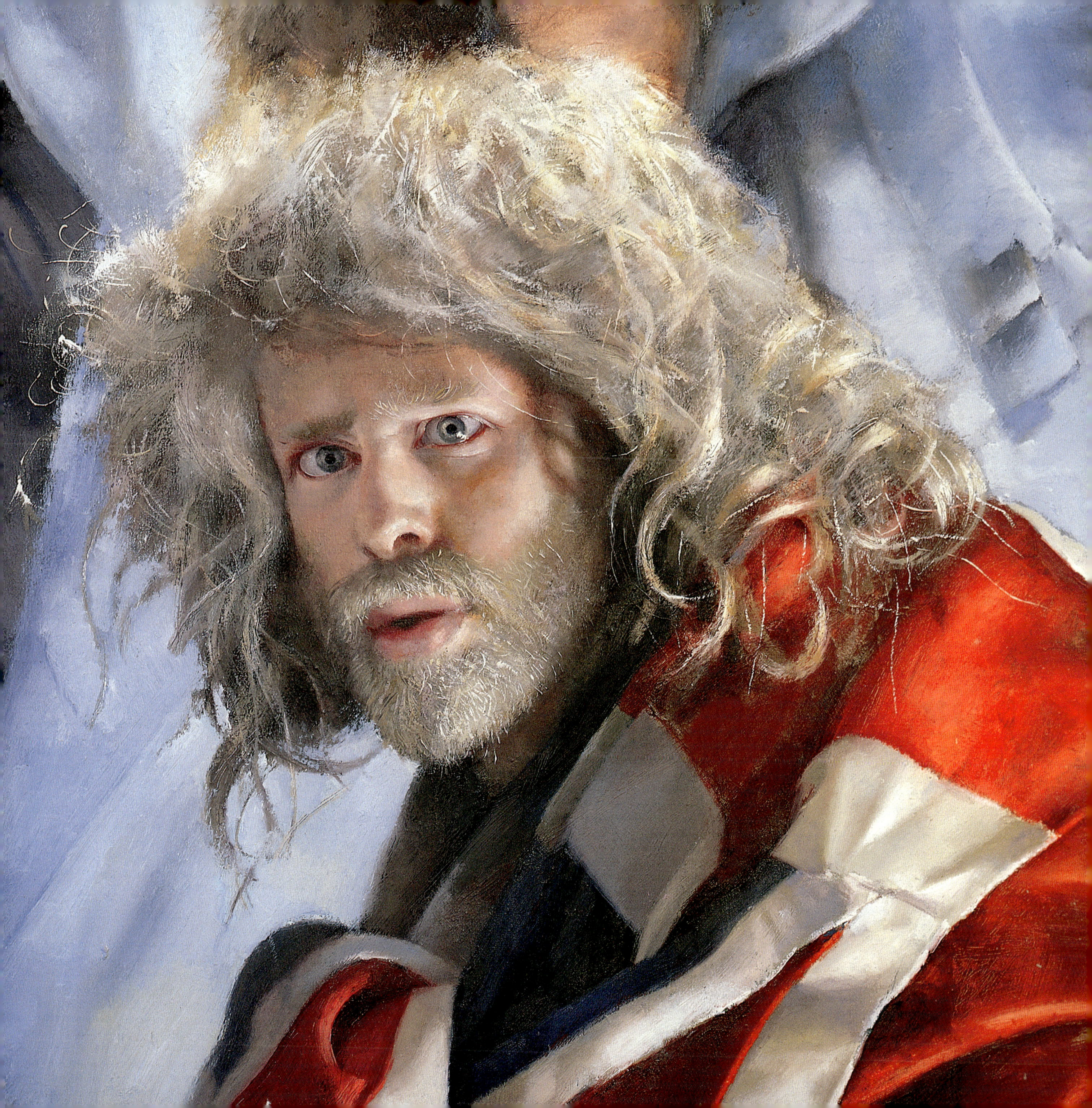

The Folly of Wise Men

R.O. Lenkiewicz

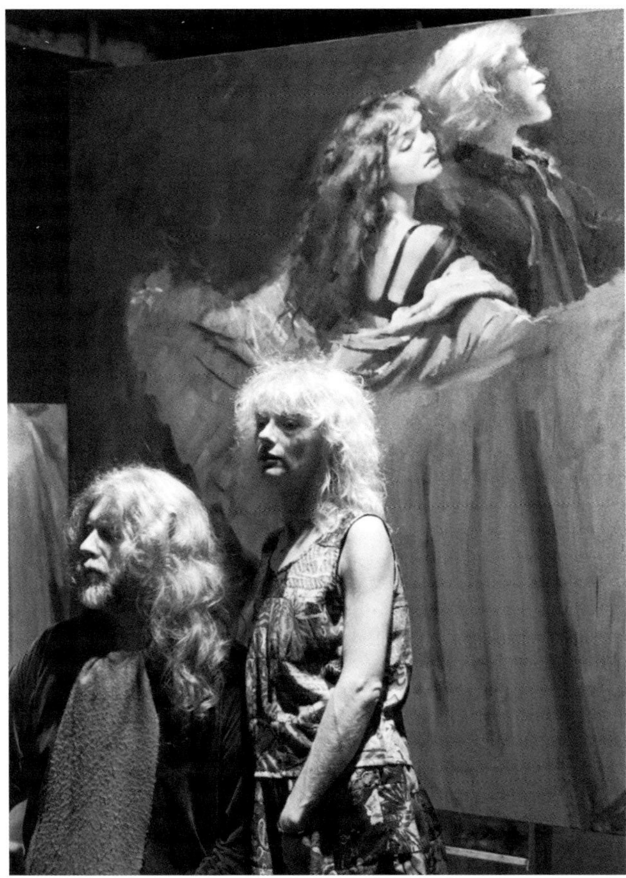

Robert with Patti Avery in the Barbican Studio, 1991. The canvas
The Painter with Karen Dancing to Mahler is seen behind.
Photo: Dr P. Stokes.

1989
The Painter With Patti Avery.
St Antony Theme.
Oil on canvas.
97 x 86 cm.

'It hath been thought a vast commendation of a painter to say his figures seem to breathe; but surely it is a much greater and nobler applause that they appear to think.'

Joseph Andrews
Preface, London 1742
HENRY FIELDING

These studies are introductory enquiries concerning three aspects of perception: 1. the relationship between one person and another; 2. philosophical considerations inspired by the mirror; 3. the 'folly of wise men'.

These studies are sketches for Project Eighteen of the Relationship Series. The large exhibition planned for the summer is on the theme, THE PAINTER WITH WOMEN: OBSERVATIONS ON THE THEME OF THE DOUBLE. (This eighteenth Project in the summer will probably be the last large-scale exhibition by Lenkiewicz in the city as he loses his studio in October in order that the handsome Georgian warehouse can be converted into another pub/club/restaurant).

Of the three issues that have preoccupied the painter in this Project, the 'folly of wise men' formula and the 'reflection' formula are significant.

The acclaimed father of Christian Monasticism was St Antony the Anchorite of Egypt. His personal struggle and eventual triumph was an epic moral tale of heroic asceticism versus the weakness of the flesh. The traditional metaphor of Lust is ironically presented in these studies with the painter as St Antony.

It need hardly be emphasised that the painter does not share St Antony's motivation. He is, however, interested in the thesis that there is no fool like an old fool.

'Reflection does not concern itself with objects themselves with a view to deriving concepts from them directly, but is that state of mind in which we first set ourselves to discover the subjective conditions under which we are able to arrive at concepts.'

Critique of Pure Reason
Tr. N. K. Smith, p. 267
IMMANUEL KANT

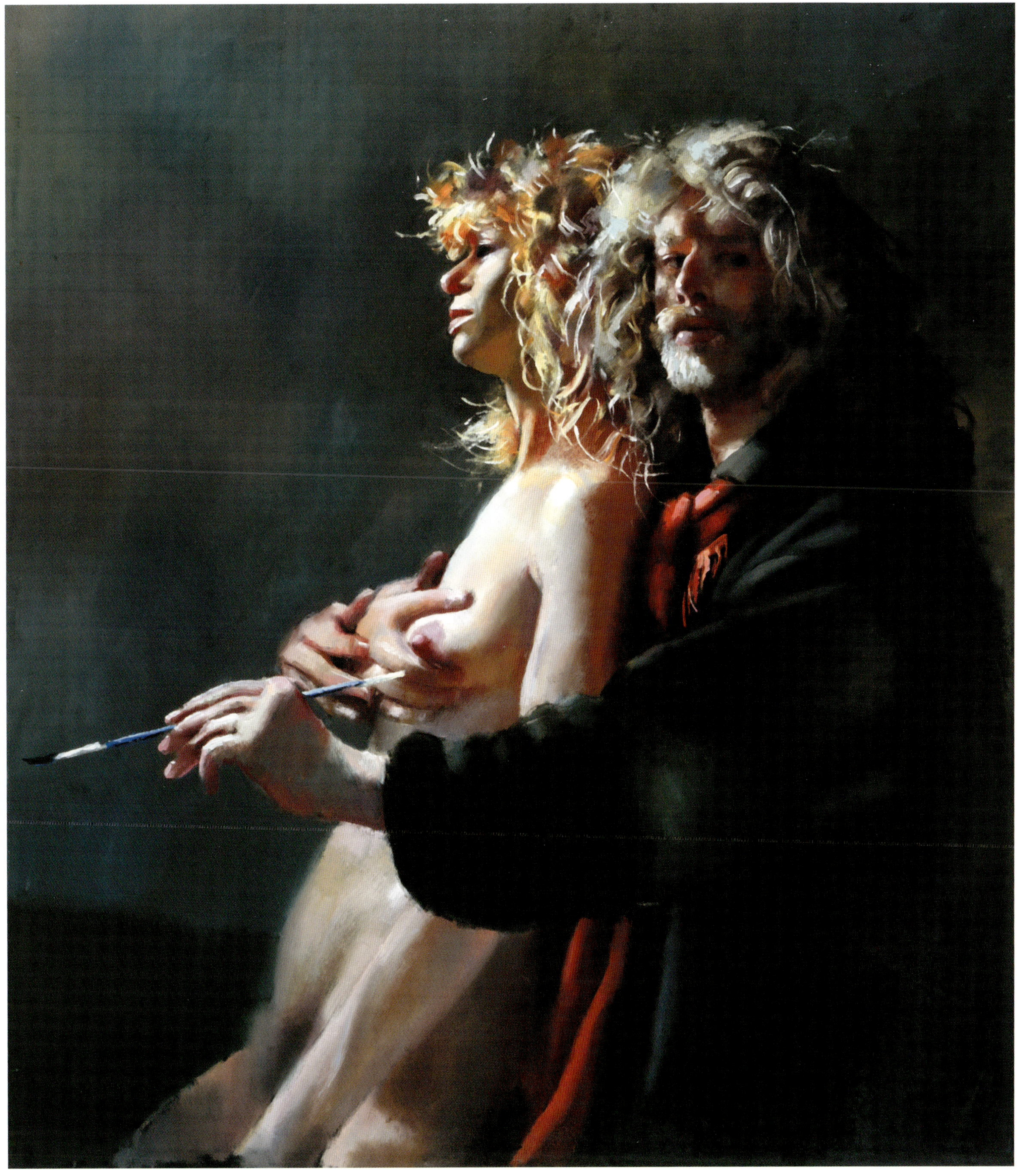

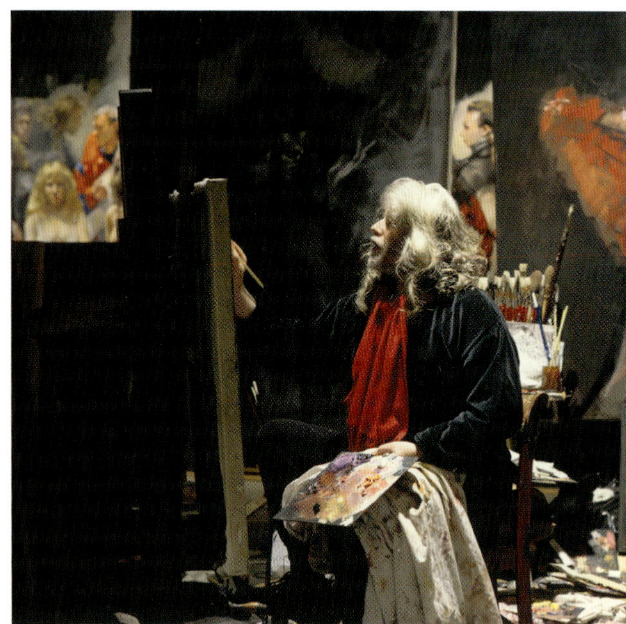

Robert Lenkiewicz in the Barbican Studio in 1993.
Photo: D. Harris.

The formula of the 'Reflection' is complex. Philosophers have been fascinated by it for centuries. From Descartes on we turn away from a straightforward consideration of objects towards a consideration of the experience in which objects are given. We thematise the subject of thought itself. Self-reflection marks the human being's rise to the rank of a subject. In Greek and Latin philosophy the term 'Reflection' has optic connotations – the mirror surface throws back light. Unlike the common notion of reflection, reflection as a philosophical concept requires that the action of reproduction also be thrown back upon itself. Where these studies are concerned the reflection formula is a metaphor for thinking.

Enshrined in our culture amidst a million ghostly truisms ... we stare into the dark, into the deepest shadows, and barely make out the diluted shape of Narcissus gazing fixedly upon the surface of the reflecting pool. He is the first artist, man transfixed by a reflection. The reflection in the mirror is the reflection of the 'real world' but the 'real world' too is the reflection of endless reflections. Voltaire once said that 'in every relationship there are a minimum of six people: you; the person talking to you; the person you think you are; the person you think they are; the person they think they are and the person they think you are.'

The reflecting surface of a mirror is an optical variant of the reflecting surface of your companion. The mirror may have one surface; had a satyr dropped a stone into Narcissus' pool his reflection would disappear like a many-faceted diamond. I look into the mirror, I speculate, I reflect upon the reflection. To reflect significantly is like flight. A view from a great height extends the reflection, it may not focus it into meaning.

One's environment and culture, one's relationships, one's passions, one's deepest and most willed intentions may be nothing more than a broken mirror.

To break a mirror brings bad luck they say, perhaps that is because a broken mirror is the closest we get to our own reality.

'We only have recourse to what is called reflection because knowledge escapes us; forgetfulness is the flight of knowledge, and reflection, by awakening a new memory in the place of the departing one, maintains knowledge in such a manner that it appears to be the same.'

The Symposium, 208c
PLATO

R.O. Lenkiewicz
*Notes to an exhibition of studies for Project 18
at the New Street Gallery, 1990*

1993
Self-Portrait as St Antony Listening.
Oil on canvas.
122 x 122 cm.

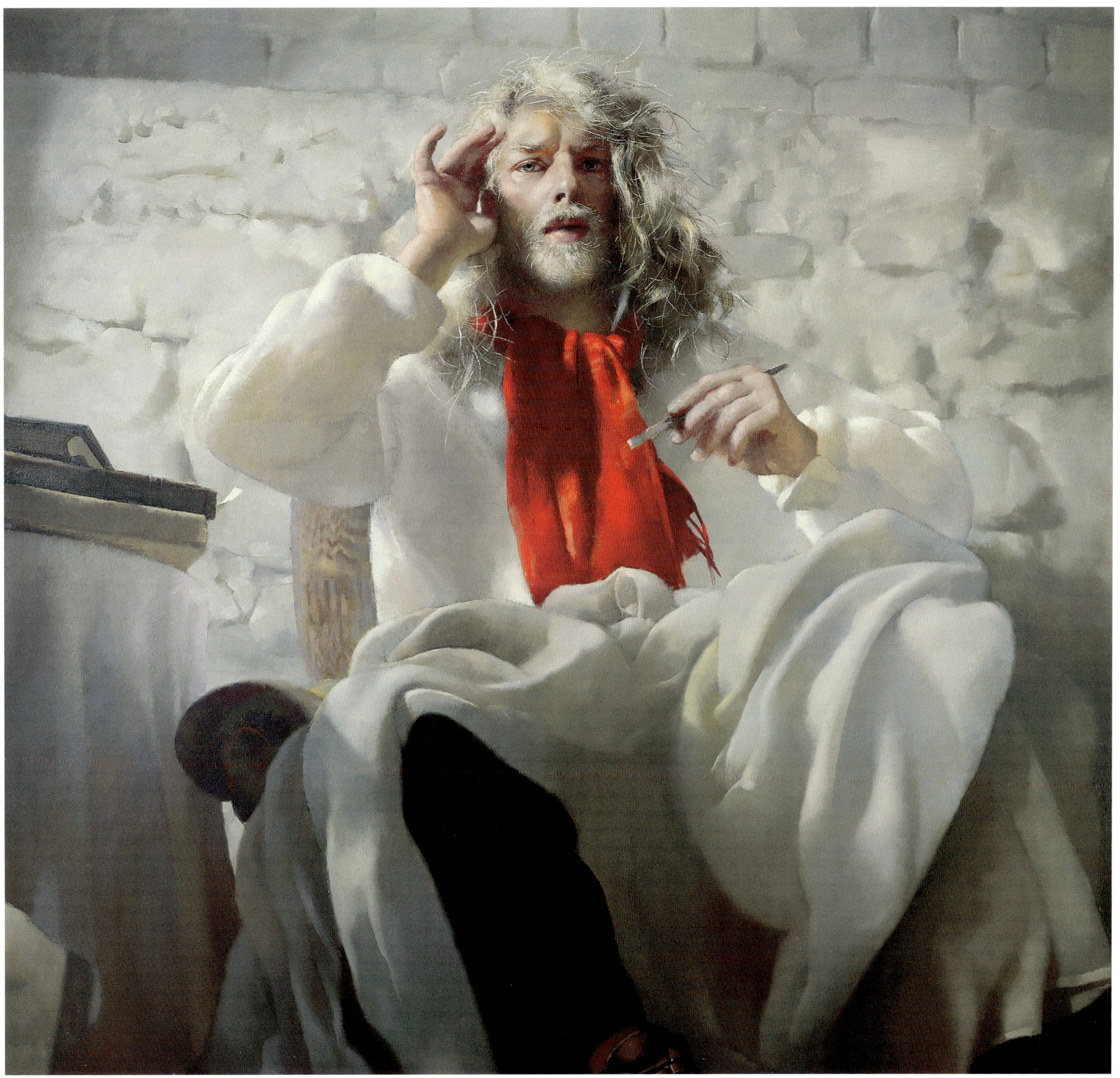

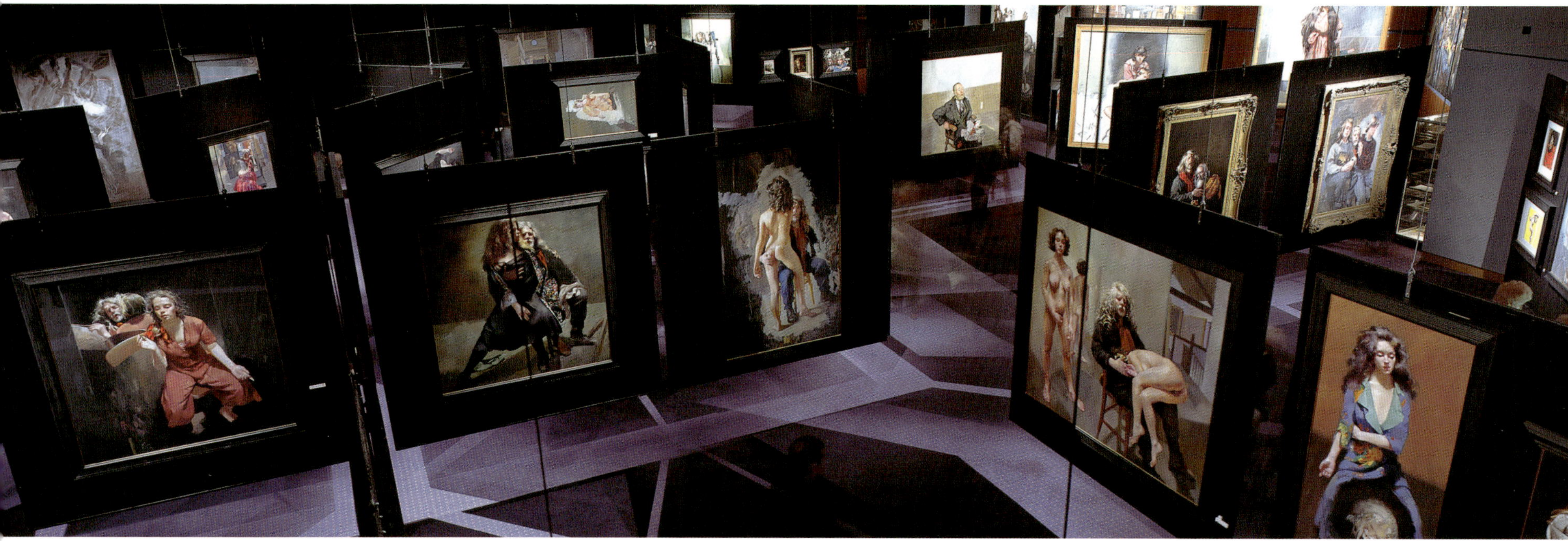

A partial showing of *The Painter With Women Project* at the ICC in January 1994. The 'Retrospective' section is seen upper right.
Photo: D. Harris.

'It's amazing that an artist will depict himself in the way that Lenkiewicz has in this picture. It's something to make you think, not just a nice thing to tone in with the wallpaper, the carpets and the curtains. I can understand that Lenkiewicz portrays himself as Pan, and this is why he's got another picture of himself copulating with a goat. And that's the story of Pan. It's just a brilliant picture!'

Visitor to the ICC exhibition
Westcountry Television film Lenkiewicz: Demon or Delight?
first transmitted 9 May 1996

1993
Self-Portrait With Cloven Hoof.
St Antony Theme.
Oil on canvas.
102 x 94 cm.

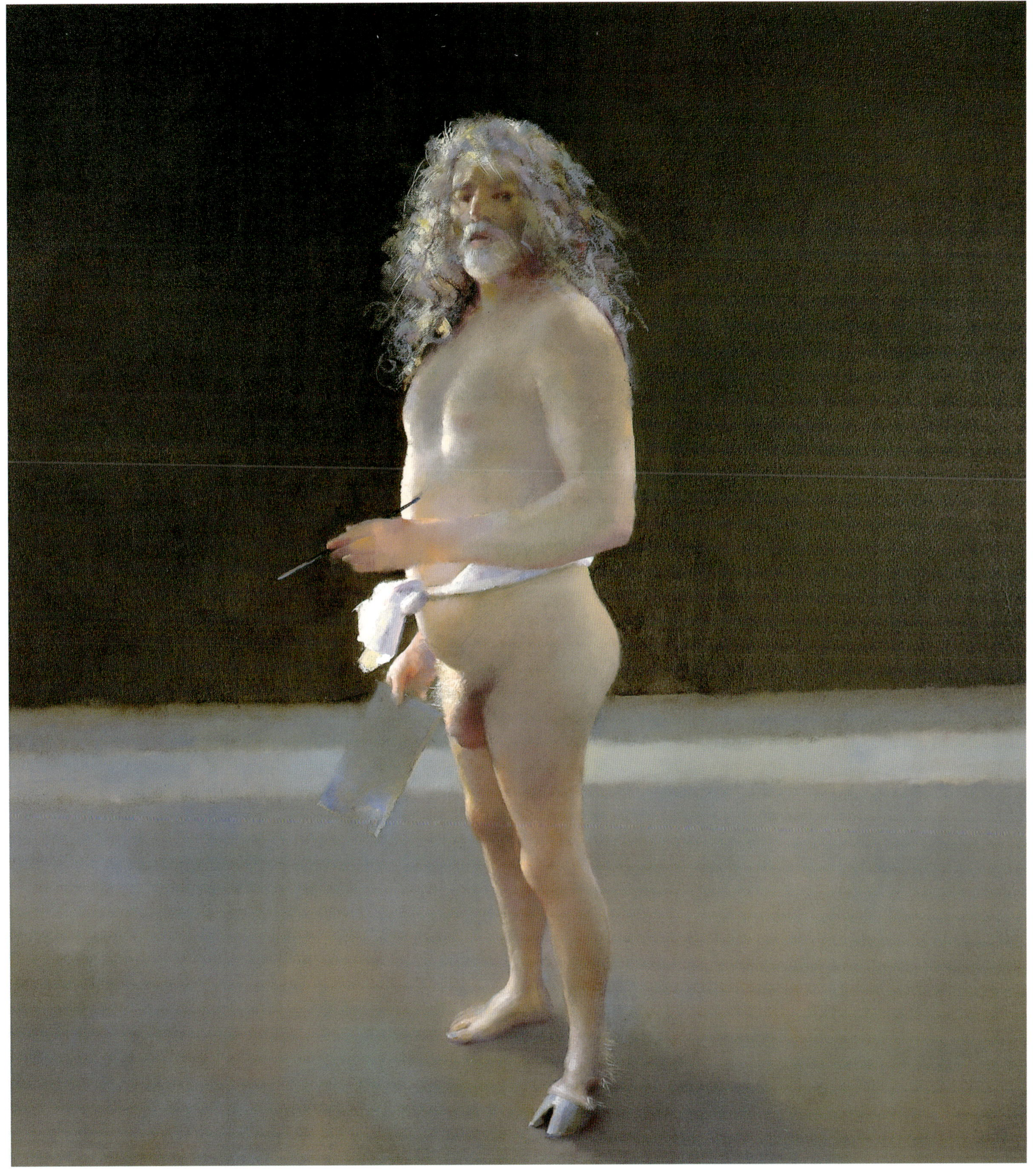

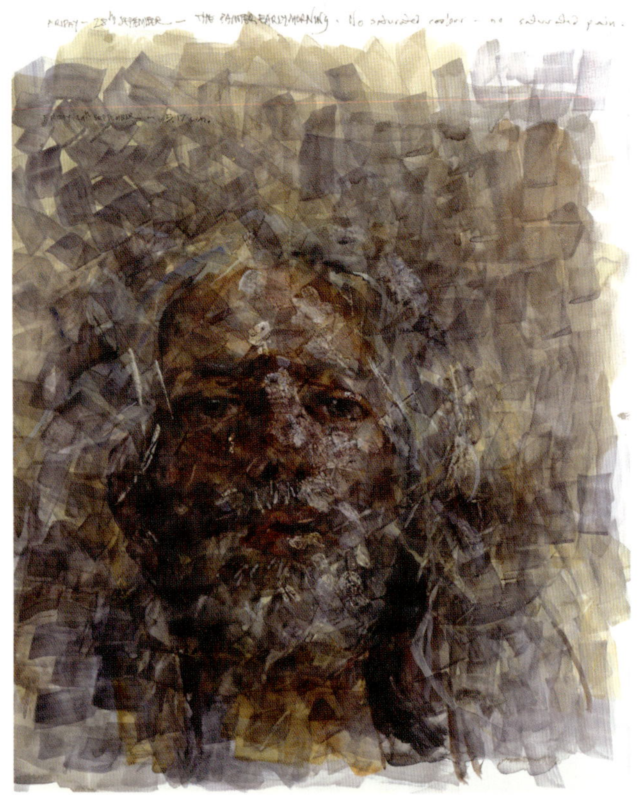

'No *Saturated Colour, No Saturated Pain* was the first of a series of paintings in oil and watercolour that Robert painted after undergoing a heart bypass operation at St Bart's Hospital in London in September 1995.

Robert took to painting at night when he couldn't sleep, the ward was quiet and he wasn't distracted by the discomfort of his surgery. At the same time he made a grid that charted rising pain and its subsequent retreat after his timed medication. He seemed interested in the very apparent physical nature of his illness and recovery.

Contrary to the interpretation that this series of paintings, as well as some of his final self-portraits, reflect his frame of mind towards the end of his life and at times of severe illness, or that the sombre palette and lack of rich colour is indicative of his psychological state, I don't believe that this is a view with which Robert himself would sympathise. This self-portrait in particular, is an attempt at a direct interpretation of his physiological experience at that exact moment (5.17 a.m. on Friday 29 September 1995); the later self-portraits are of a man getting older, succumbing to ill health. This may appear a face-value way of seeing the paintings but it is one which I think Robert himself, with his determination to understand human nature and behaviour from a physiological point of view, would hold.'

Anna Navas, 2008

1995
The Painter, Early Morning. No Saturated Colour, No Saturated Pain.
Watercolour on paper.
37 x 29 cm.

1995
The Painter With Anna.
Oil on canvas.
121 x 119 cm.

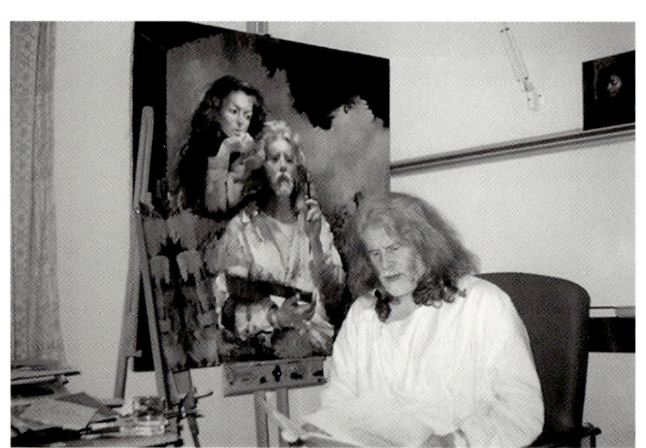

Robert Lenkiewicz in Derriford Hospital, Plymouth, in 1995.

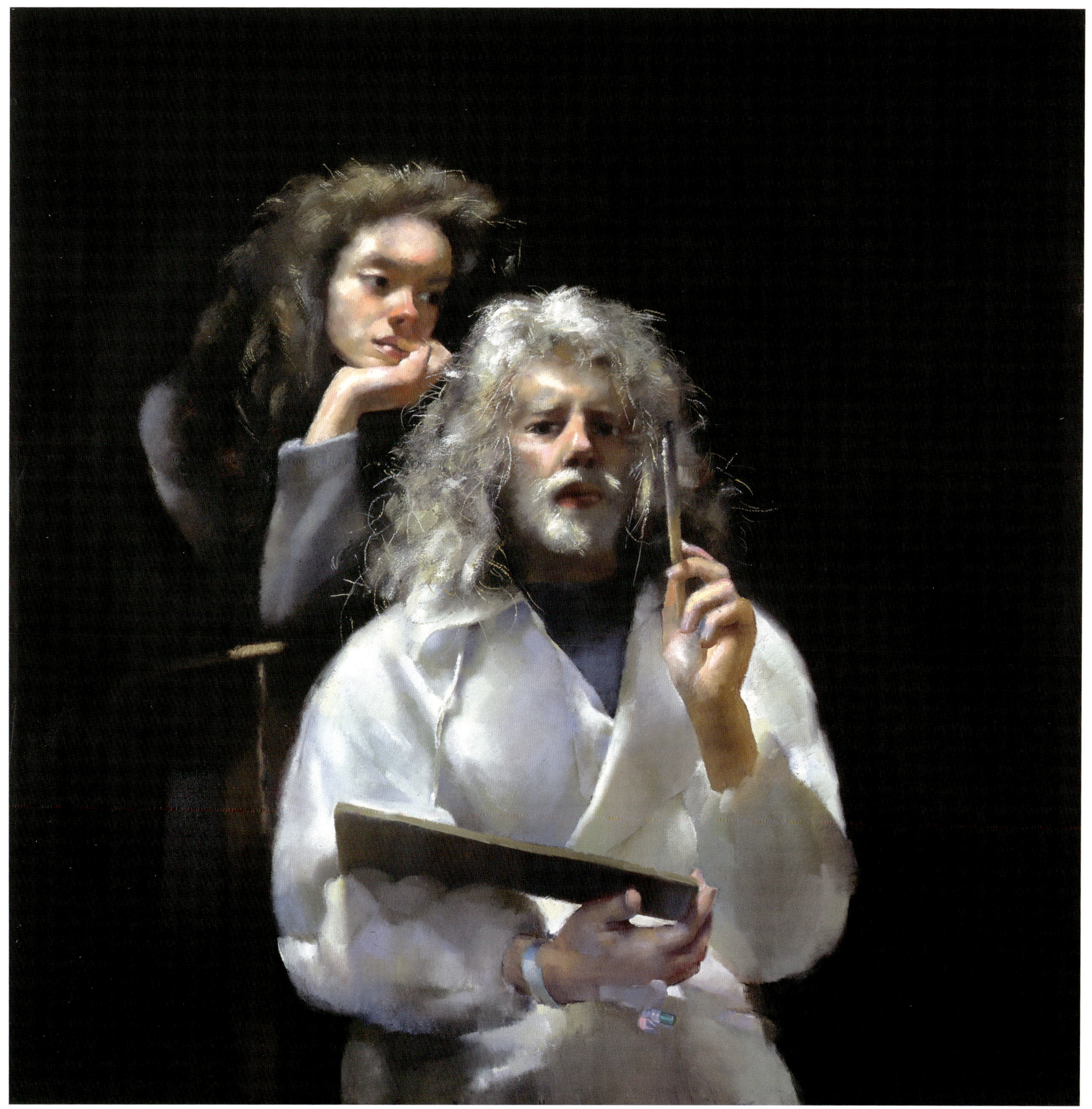

PROJECT 19: LANDSCAPE – THE PAINTER AS ST JEROME
1995

'All human enterprise seems to evaporate into the vapours that we inhale and exhale by seeing. Seeing is eating; our visual mouth can swallow universes, exhale the starry night. When we are moved, we are filled. To be touched by things is to be made smaller, to be diminished. In one aesthetic mood we ride clouds and leapfrog oaks, in another we sleep beneath a leaf and nestle with insects. Space is a state of mind, agoraphobic and claustrophobic. We are strangely haunted by events that are innocent of themselves, we do not cry "Show off!" to Nature. We are silenced into meditative irony, diminished and expanded, an elastic perception of minutiae one moment and infinity the next.'

R.O. Lenkiewicz
Notes on the Landscape Theme

RL: I went to see the cottage on the estuary and the moment I saw it I knew I would do a whole Project on that. I had the idea for a Project called *Earth, Air, Fire and Water*, but then I changed my mind and did a little of everything. Some early studies have been shown, but I have in mind a large exhibition of landscapes all centred on that place. A lot of that Project related to feelings about isolation. I had a lot of intense times, particularly the night paintings.

The *Landscape Project* exhibition poster shows the intended subtext of the theme – *The Painter as St Jerome* – 'an enquiry into the relationship between natural forces and a single person.' *Photo*: Dr P. Stokes.

1995
The Painter in the Wind, 3.50 a.m., July.
Oil on board.
51 x 43 cm.

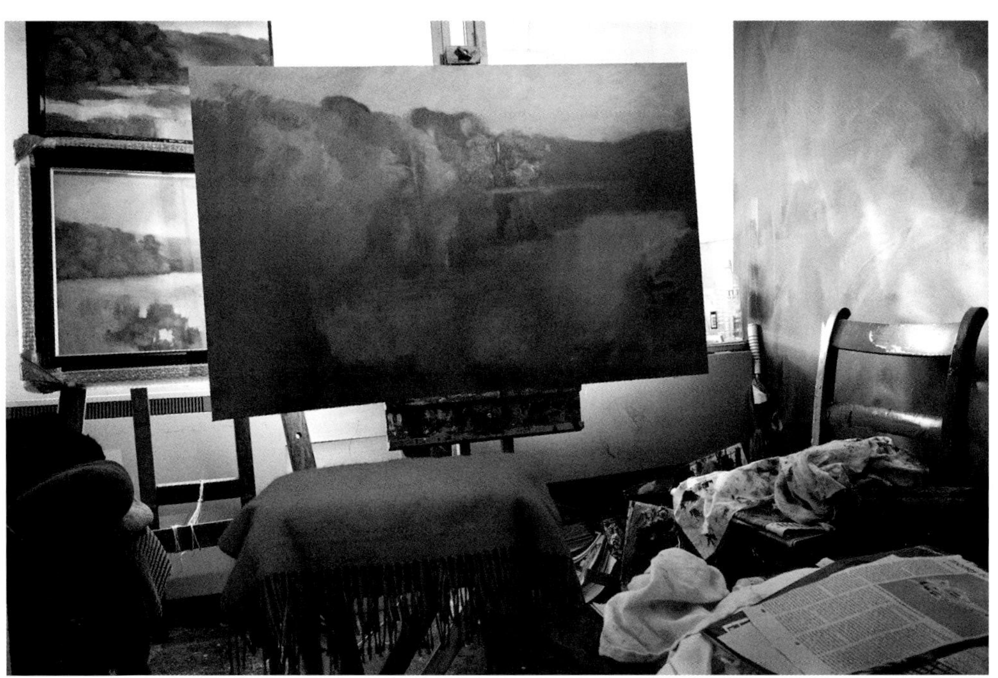

Work in progress for the *Landscape Project* in 1995 at the Mudbank Lake studio near Yealmpton in South Devon. *Photo*: Dr P. Stokes.

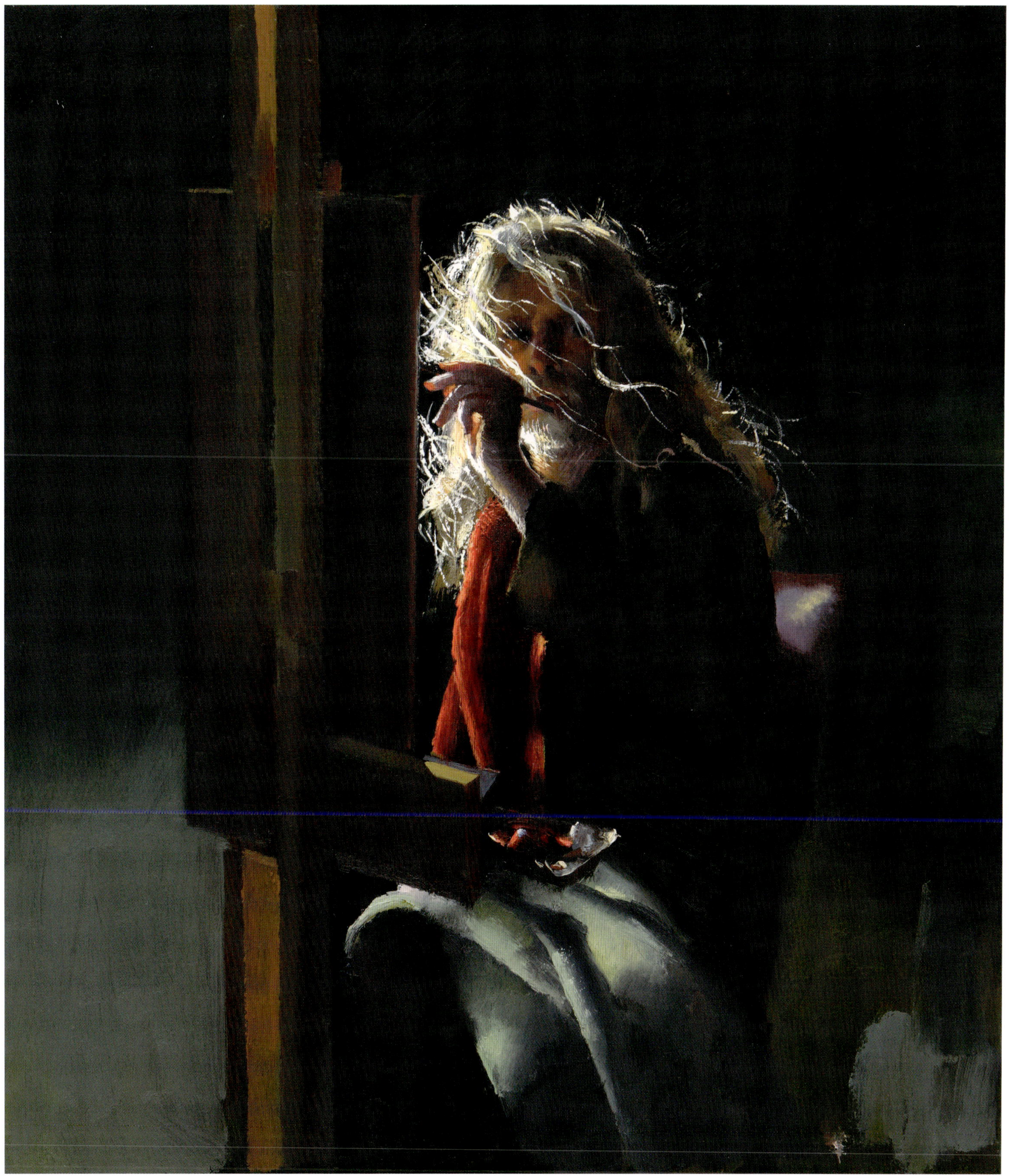

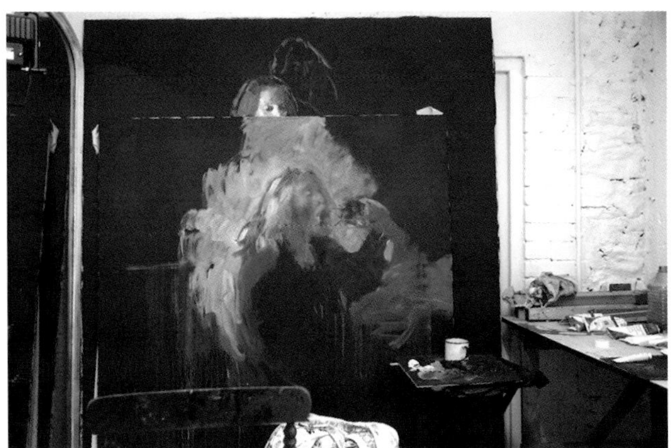

Work in progress on the theme of 'swallowing time' at the Theology Building studio, 2002. *Photo*: Dr P. Stokes.

*c.*2000
Self-Portrait With Hourglass.
Oil on canvas.
110 x 61 cm.

'I don't personally look for happiness in the end, I look for interest. I don't think that life is about being happy. I think living is to be interested and to be stimulated. One's longer dead than one's alive, and everything passes. I'm middle-aged now, too many cheeseburgers, been ill, better now, more sensible diet, working hard. In my mind I've got five or ten years; quite adequate. No objections to living for a thousand years, but quite happy with five or ten, and no objections to dying.

It's a clever trick, it is truly an art, to maintain the sensation that life is extraordinary and inexplicable, without a desire to hunt it down for truths, all of which will pass. And the feeling of enrichment, of feeling significant to oneself, without being too much of a public nuisance, is, I think, one of the profoundest tricks to learn in this extraordinary business of living.'

R.O. Lenkiewicz
Remarks from the stage of Plymouth Theatre Royal
An Evening with Lenkiewicz, *Sunday 28 April 1996*

'This house [Priory Road] was known as Death House long before I ever came here. Sometimes they called it the Witch's House, but mainly Death House, and the reason must have been this skull, which is placed over the door, with a laurel leaf crown – 'Death succeeds, Death is king.' The intention is that I will be buried down there, along the lines of this design [Robert unfolds a plan, showing the proposed "chapel" building and tunnel in vertical elevation and sagittal section].

The plan is that the small hut, which I call St Antony's Hut, down there, can be entered; you go down the steps, into a tunnel that is structured underneath. I will be buried quite innocuously under a slab, under there, and anyone else can be buried there as well. All are welcome. And then up through here, up these steps, into the large studio in the house there. Up through there, and that room will be a huge reliquary box ... gold structured frames, paintings some twenty or twenty-five feet high, dealing with the theme of Life and Death.

The intention is that this place which I'm so fond of, so quiet and atmospheric ... the public could come here, but not to see a Lenkiewicz mausoleum or where I'm buried – they won't be able to see that very clearly. The tunnel will be carved, will have artefacts and paintings related to the Death theme, and it will be seen to have almost a meditative function, for people to remember that they will die: a memento mori.'

R.O. Lenkiewicz
Westcountry Television film Lenkiewicz: Demon or Delight?
first transmitted 9 May 1996

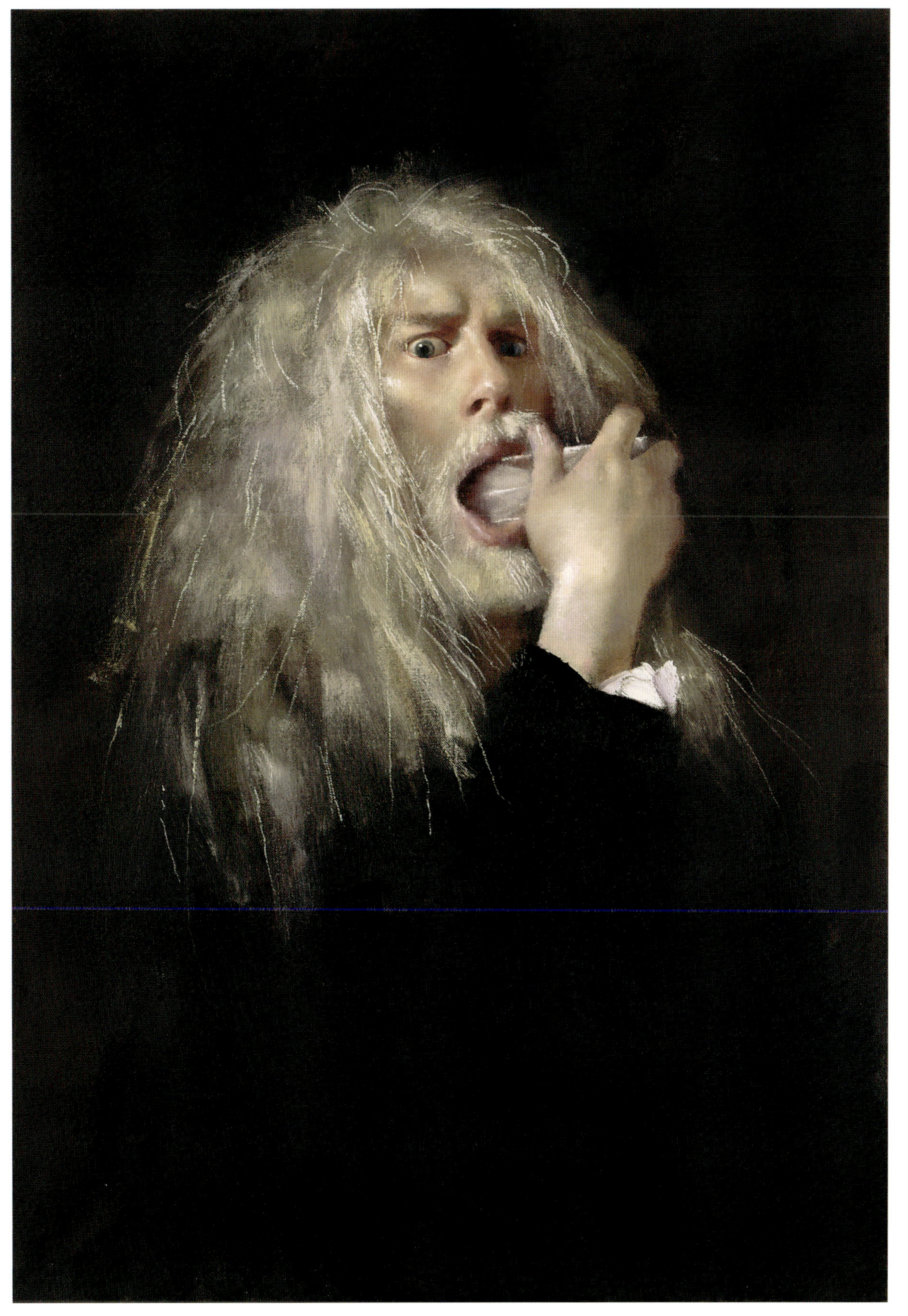

Robert Lenkiewicz: Ideas and Libraries

N.J. Fox

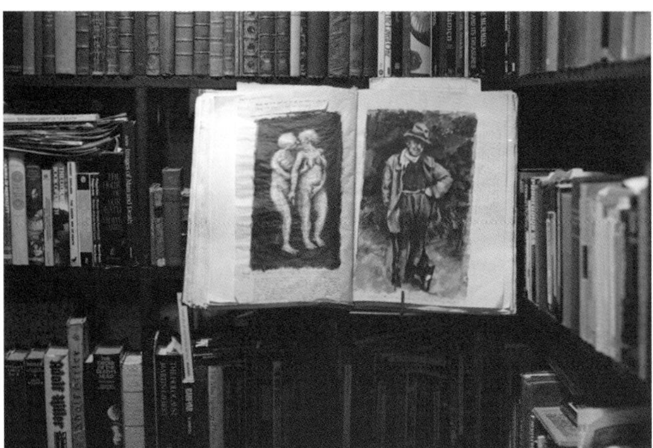

Death Room: The *Old Age Project Notebook* in the library of the Barbican Studio. *Photo*: Dr P. Stokes.

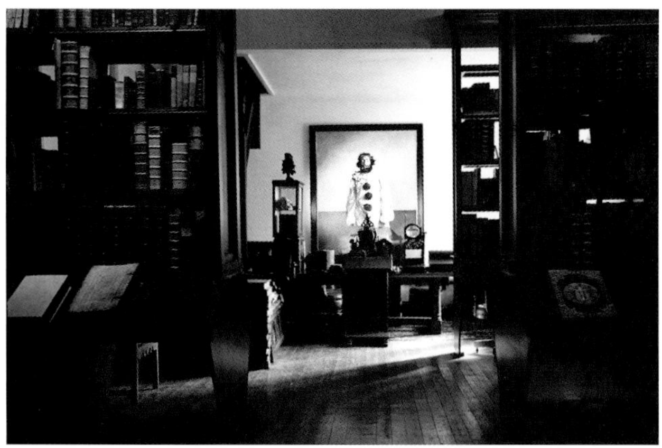

The Philosophy Library in St Saviour's Church in 2001. It is based on the Duke Humfrey library of the Bodleian, part of the University of Oxford. *Photo*: Dr P. Stokes.

2000

Self-Portrait Holding Philippe Aries'
In The Hour of Our Death.

Oil on canvas.

110 x 61 cm.

What does a painter need with a library amounting to 25,000 books? I had almost exclusive use of Robert Lenkiewicz's St Saviour's library while I worked on a doctoral thesis on philosophy and mysticism. For more than three years I sat at my desk on the first floor of this converted church, surrounded by a thousand antiquarian books on philosophy. Downstairs there were a further five thousand modern books on the subject. The gaze of John Locke looked down on me from his portrait; the skeletal remains of an executed witch kept me company. The only sounds were the muted cries that came from the seagulls that nested around the observation tower. This was my home from home, my 'own' library. I was left undisturbed, but for occasional visits from Lenkiewicz himself, who would often, rather apologetically, ask me if I wouldn't mind translating a bit of Latin for him. A small price to pay: if it had not been for him granting me access to his private collection, I would have had to make frequent visits to the British Library in London. There, you request a book and wait an hour, maybe more – if the title is available. Whereas at St Saviour's I had only to walk a few feet to lift the tome I needed from its shelf, perhaps one on 17th-century kabbalism.

Lenkiewicz had another library. This one was adjacent to his main studio and was extended over three floors. The ground floor consisted of three interconnected windowless rooms, which were lined entirely with books. Here was the excellent art history and biography collection of some five thousand books, and the very strong collection of antiquarian and modern books on occult philosophy (a variant of Neo-Platonic metaphysics that was revived during the Renaissance), which amounted to three thousand items.

On the second floor was a room called the 'death room', which contained books on old age, gerontology, melancholy, suicide and eschatology (theories of the afterlife). There was also a large section on the Holocaust and Nazism. Artefacts housed in here included original transcripts from the Nuremburg war trials, Nazi memorabilia, human skulls and other body parts, and there was the embalmed corpse of the tramp Diogenes that was kept in a special drawer.

Also on the second floor was the 'witchcraft room'. Here was possibly the finest collection of antiquarian books in private hands in Europe. Amongst the nine hundred items on demonology and witchcraft, there were a dozen editions of the notorious Kramer and Sprenger *Malleus Maleficarum* (*The Hammer of Witches*).

A further room on this level housed books on sociological and psychological studies about the nature of sex and desire. On the third floor were modern works of literature and biographies of authors and musicians.

So, what does a painter need with a library amounting to 25,000 books? Over the years that I knew Robert Lenkiewicz, and through conversations we had, I learnt of the key ideas that he was interested in, how they determined many of

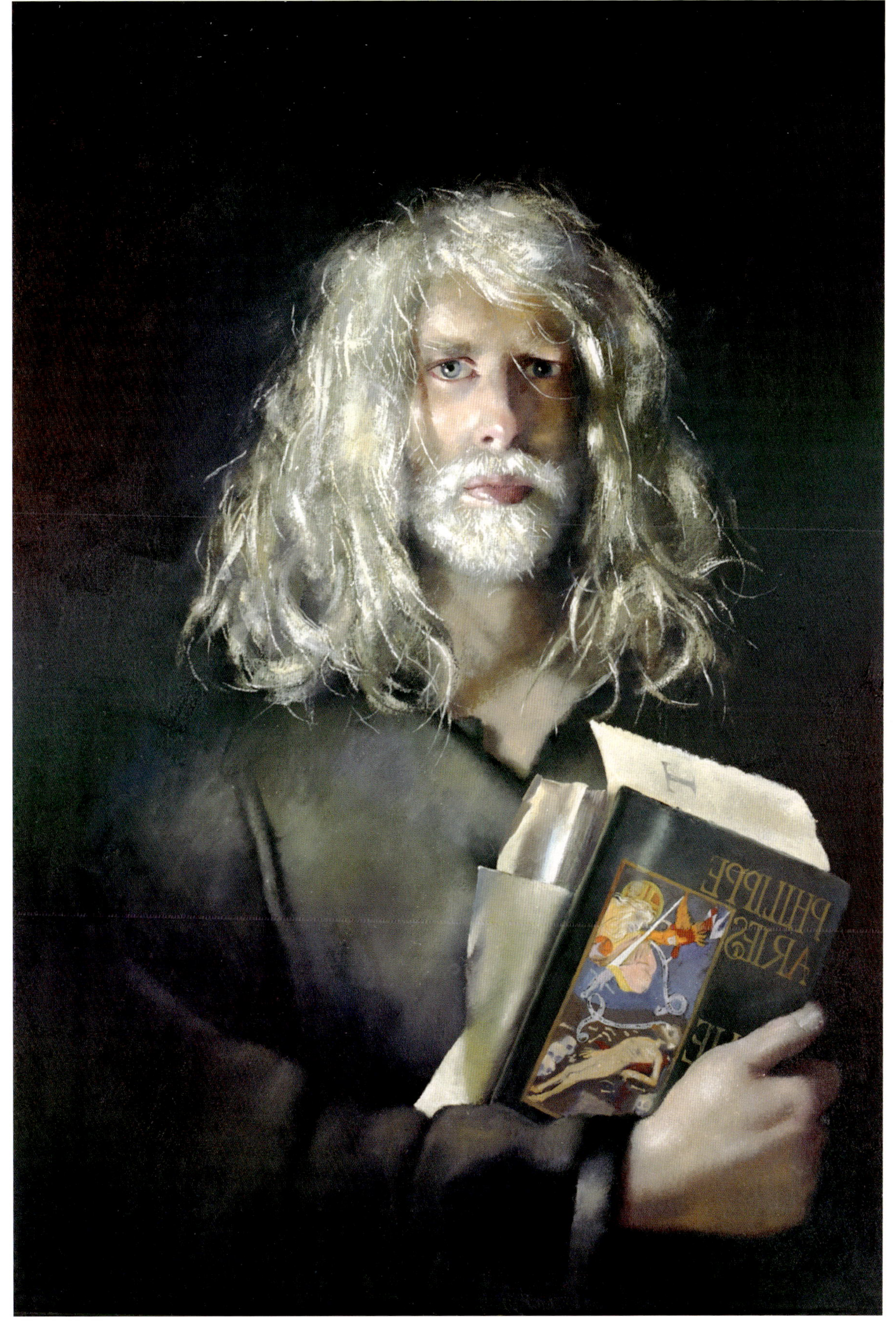

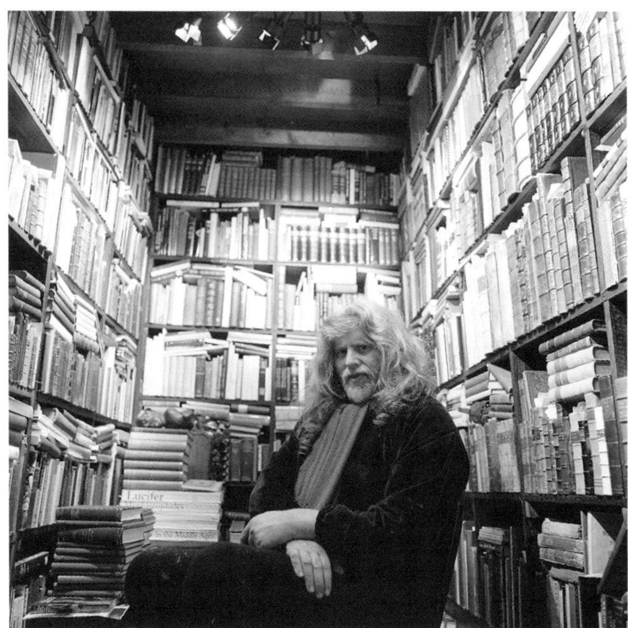

Robert Lenkiewicz in the Metaphysics Room of his private library in 1991. *Photo*: S. Hemmings

*"Book dealers are a bit like heroin dealers.
In fact, they're not a bit like them, they're just
like them! And a book collector like myself is
just like a heroin addict. I don't think there's
any difference – not physiologically – and I'm as
susceptible as the next."*

R.O. Lenkiewicz

the painting projects that he worked on, how they were the basis of his research into certain sociological issues, and how they were ultimately the *raison d'être* for much of his painting and book collecting. These ideas were similar to many of the concepts that I was dealing with in my own work. I will now set out what I think was Lenkiewicz's principal philosophical idea – an idea that he termed 'aesthetic fascism'.

This idea is the one that we, as human beings, do not choose our desires; that we do not choose our actions or the ideas that we hold as truths. Lenkiewicz early on his career had painted many down-and-outs, and he had spent a lot of time in their company. They were all addicted to alcohol, many were addicted to narcotics. In listening to their accounts of what it felt like to crave alcohol when deprived of it, Lenkiewicz perceived a close resemblance to his own feelings of jealousy, the feeling of being deprived of one whom one loves: jealousy as a withdrawal symptom similar to that of the alcoholic. This was the seed of the idea that perhaps all our feelings are addictions: cravings which we cannot switch off any more than we can choose to switch them on: they simply take possession of us. Your desire, your craving, say for another person, is essentially a selfish one: your love, your desire, is your own desire: it is not a selfless, impersonal, admiration at a distance of some supposed objective characteristic of the other. So when you love someone, you are not bestowing a gift of selfless objective praise for which the other is somehow then in your debt. And if someone loves or physically desires you, you have no debt to them, you have no need to feel obliged towards them, to accommodate them in some way: they simply crave you according to their own unchosen desires in the same way as any other addict craves the object of his desire. The intellect, reason, is powerless in the face of such desires: hence many people remain in violent relationships despite their intellectual knowledge that the relationship should end.

It is your aesthetic impulses which unconditionally tell you what is good and beautiful, what you crave for; and they tell you what is bad and ugly, what you are repulsed by. This uncompromising judging of other people and things is quite authoritarian: we are fascistic in this sense: our aesthetic experiences are fascistic. Political fascism is thus simply the same process manifest in groups of individual people: the group is possessed of certain likes and dislikes: it cannot choose, intellectually or any other way, which characteristics to be attracted to, and it cannot choose to switch these likes and dislikes off or on. Apart from his own observations and personal experiences, Lenkiewicz found intellectual support in the writings of the philosopher Friedrich Nietzsche.

Aesthetic fascism is not restricted simply to our bodily and emotional desires: it equally applies to our mental desires. You hold the beliefs that you do without choice: you have a mental aesthetic impulse that unconditionally tells you what is good and true, and what is bad and false: which ideas and theories you are attracted to and which repel you. You are equally fascistic in your holding some belief to be a true one as you are in holding some object to be a beautiful one. In the same way as drug addicts or love addicts can be violent in their pursuit of what they crave, so too can truth addicts: in geopolitical terms we can see different truth systems at war: e.g. in Reformation and Counter-Reformation, in the Axis of Evil, etc, etc. Lenkiewicz termed all such systems of truth 'fanatical belief systems'.

Lenkiewicz was asked whether an understanding of the addictive fascistic nature of love would cause the associated edifice of rights and obligations to crumble. He answered this way:

> Once one establishes for oneself that it is an *aesthetic* experience that one is undergoing and not something else, then I think that a number of behaviour patterns could evaporate. I don't expect human behaviour to change; neither do I need it to. I simply expect that a time will come when people could not reasonably make irrational claims for their feeling or one's responsibility towards it. I have difficulty feeling that I have rights due me from people I may bump into in life. That kind of silliness fades away with age anyway – I don't see why it isn't possible to have that information earlier on … But I do feel that by not being so emotionally convinced that whatever 'truth' a person feels that they are linked with is the case, or whatever person they feel they are linked with owes them anything, it's reasonable to entertain the notion that they're likely to be calmer and to recognise that life is a tragedy, but a very liveable tragedy, and to be glad when they're glad.

So if people could be brought round to see that truth and love are not reasons to go to war either in a personal relationship or in geopolitical terms they may not act any differently but at least they will be more accepting of life – as a tragedy, in the Greek sense – in the Dionysian sense of Nietzsche.

So we can see Lenkiewicz's work as displaying the tragedy of the human condition. And he did this in three stages:

1) He depicted important issues about human life in paintings that impress and move the public – and, importantly, in ways that are accessible to the greatest number of people (and not only to highbrows or the cultural elite). Usually these paintings were straightforward portraits of individuals affected by an issue; sometimes non-representational works would depict the issue in a more illustrational way.

2) He accompanied his exhibitions on a certain theme with notes that explained the presence of aesthetic fascism, and often with notes by the sitters themselves, who had had direct experience of the issue.

3) He collected books that related to aesthetic fascism: either books that are about it (such as philosophy, the sociology and psychology of sex and relationships) or books that are examples of it, i.e. of fanatical belief systems (such as theology, occult philosophy, Nazism and witchcraft – of which Kramer and Sprenger is in some ways an epitome, being both an example of a theological fascism and of a relationship fascism: the violence of men towards women).

Lenkiewicz's library was thus the intellectual complement to his painting endeavour, and he hoped that it would serve as a facility for those wishing to study aesthetic fascism and, thereby, help to promote the recognition of its existence in human life.

The first project that falls under the scope of aesthetic fascism dealt with, amongst others, the addiction to alcohol: the Vagrancy Project. There were many projects dealing with aesthetic fascism in personal relationships: *Death & the Maiden, Love and Romance, Love and Mediocrity, Jealousy, Orgasm, Sexual Behaviour, The Painter with Women* and, *in summa, Addictive Behaviour*.

There were, of course, projects not related directly to the aesthetic fascism idea, but which were related to the 'tragedy of life' and, as such, became objects of study by Lenkiewicz – old age, suicide, death, and even, as he saw it, education.

I had had the advantage of working in and breathing the artistic and intellectual atmosphere that had filled the microcosm that Lenkiewicz had created. It is such a shame that this was not to last, that others would not be able to enjoy what I had. And yet, the reason for the implosion of this little world was none other than – aesthetic fascism itself: the addiction to buying books and the inevitable bankruptcy; the addiction to one man's personality and the inevitable subverting of the entrustment to posterity of that world of books and paintings; and the addiction to material wealth and the inevitable vampirism that descended upon Lenkiewicz's estate. Yet if you embrace Lenkiewicz's key ideas then you must also accept that this tragedy was a necessary one: how could the feelings and the actions of all those involved ever have been otherwise?

RL: I just wanted to observe what it was about human physiology that would become dependent on another human being. It took me some years to draw the conclusion, rightly or wrongly, that one can't claim that it's the other person; the only claim that can really be made is a description of the victim's own physiology – that is what they're experiencing. When one identifies the cause of that distress as being the other person, there one enters into areas of mistaken identity and thoughtlessness, brutishness and fascism.

RL: I just thought 'what is the next most relevant theme that relates to the business of living?' and there weren't very many of them. My aim was to present information on sociological issues that were common to pretty well all people and I didn't think that there was a more responsible line of enquiry. I didn't think there was an act of research that was more significant than looking into those issues that relate to human behaviour, and really the background to that in my mind was the type of reading that I had of the work of Rembrandt.

Although there were many painters who wore themselves on their sleeves in image after image, right through to contemporary times, there were few that made the mark, the stain, the scrape and scrape on a bit of canvas, in the way that Rembrandt did, particularly in the late work. Something like the Kenwood *Self-Portrait*, *The Jewish Bride* in the Rijksmuseum, the *Bathsheba at Her Bath* in the Louvre.

I remember that as a student I used to call it 'ethical paint'. This notion that somehow suffering, and sometimes joy, but suffering more, would imprint itself from the way the paint was laid on the canvas. Nothing to do with the image being represented, nothing to do even with the painter's intellectual and emotional intentions, and nothing to do with the culture of the time – just the physical mark that is made, perhaps like the kind of mark that's made on a wall when somebody has been shot by a firing squad and the hands scrape down through his own blood.

But one really has to be very wary of a kind of etymological approach towards marks, as though they're some inherent language and that as each person's set of marks start to develop and mature they're uniquely that person's. I'm not sure about that. I look at paintings, particularly some contemporary painters, and you see this mark's like so and so's or that mark's like so and so's. I'm not sure about individuating the mark too much; it can sometimes be a cultural time-trap. I think what separates marks most intensely is suffering. If there's any tragedy in life it is that people learn through pain far more effectively than they learn through pleasure. We hardly learn anything through pleasure.

2002
Self-Portrait: The Painter in Hospital.
Oil on canvas.
67 x 72 cm.

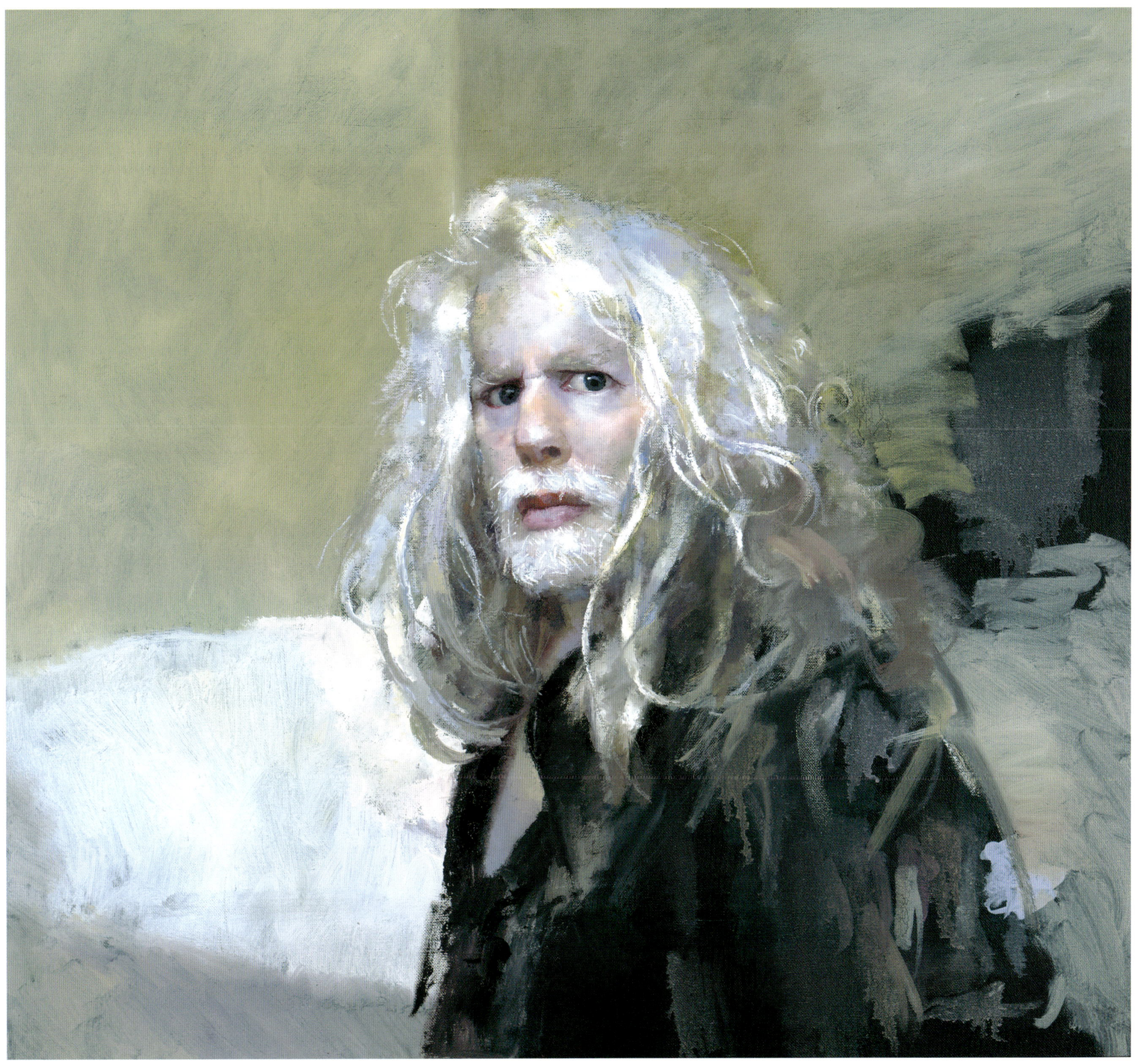

RL: I can remember at thirteen or fourteen I was reading through the New Testament quite carefully, and I came across a phrase in St Matthew, 'And Jesus loved John best.' And I remember thinking, 'Ah, one's not supposed to love one human being any more than another.' And of course we're all familiar with the Renaissance 'Last Suppers' and pretty-boy John lying on Jesus's breast at the point of betrayal.

It's an odd notion that your gurus and your wise men should prefer one person to another. It seems to me that if one loves everybody equally one has to be aesthetically dead. You strive to have no preference, but the moment you prefer anything you are undergoing an aesthetic experience; it's not a *moral* issue. 'I like that music' or 'I like that wallpaper more than that'; 'I like those trousers more than that'; 'I like that idea more than that'; 'I like that person more than that'. These are *aesthetic* decisions. *'And Jesus loved John best'* – to be aesthetically dead seems to me the first credential for sainthood.

Monica: I took him to see the Birtwhistle opera, *The Last Supper*, in Plymouth in 2001. The stage was split horizontally, with a contemporary 'Last Supper' going on below. But Christ and the Apostles had come back through time to make comment on the present day. Above were mime artists in tableaux of Renaissance paintings like the 'Stations of the Cross' and the 'Crucifixion'. Robert always used to say that the image of Christ crucified was the greatest symbol ever invented by mankind.

It was a staggering Glyndebourne performance. We were both struck dumb by it; when we came out neither of us could even talk. He said he was determined to paint his own version of *The Last Supper*. That's where he got the idea. He asked me to get together music to listen to whilst painting it.

Overleaf:

2002
The Last Supper (unfinished).
Oil on canvas.
198 x 426 cm.

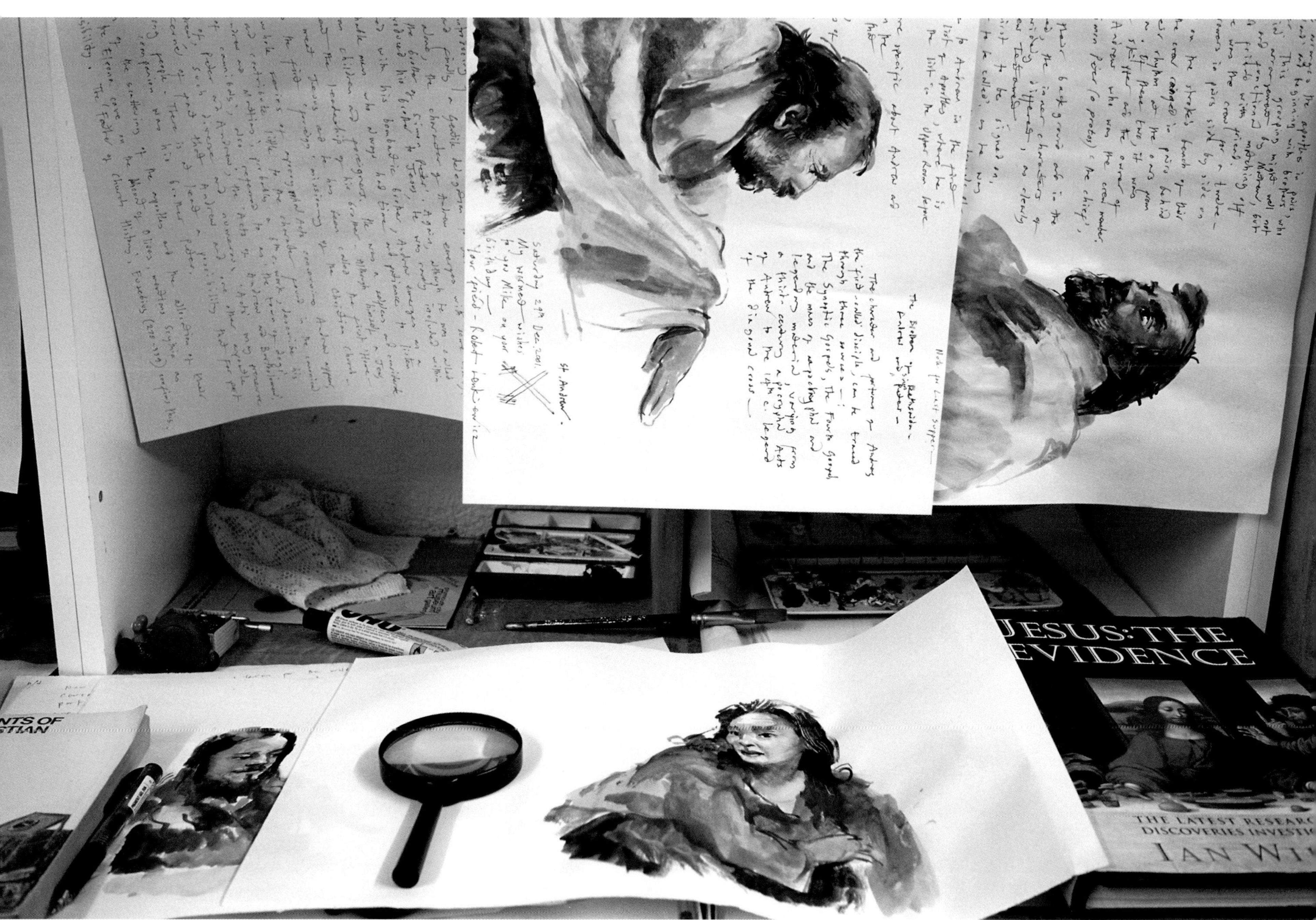

Notes and sketches for *The Last Supper* showing pages on St Andrew and Magdalene. Lenkiewicz intended to appear as Judas Iscariot. *Photo*: Dr P. Stokes.

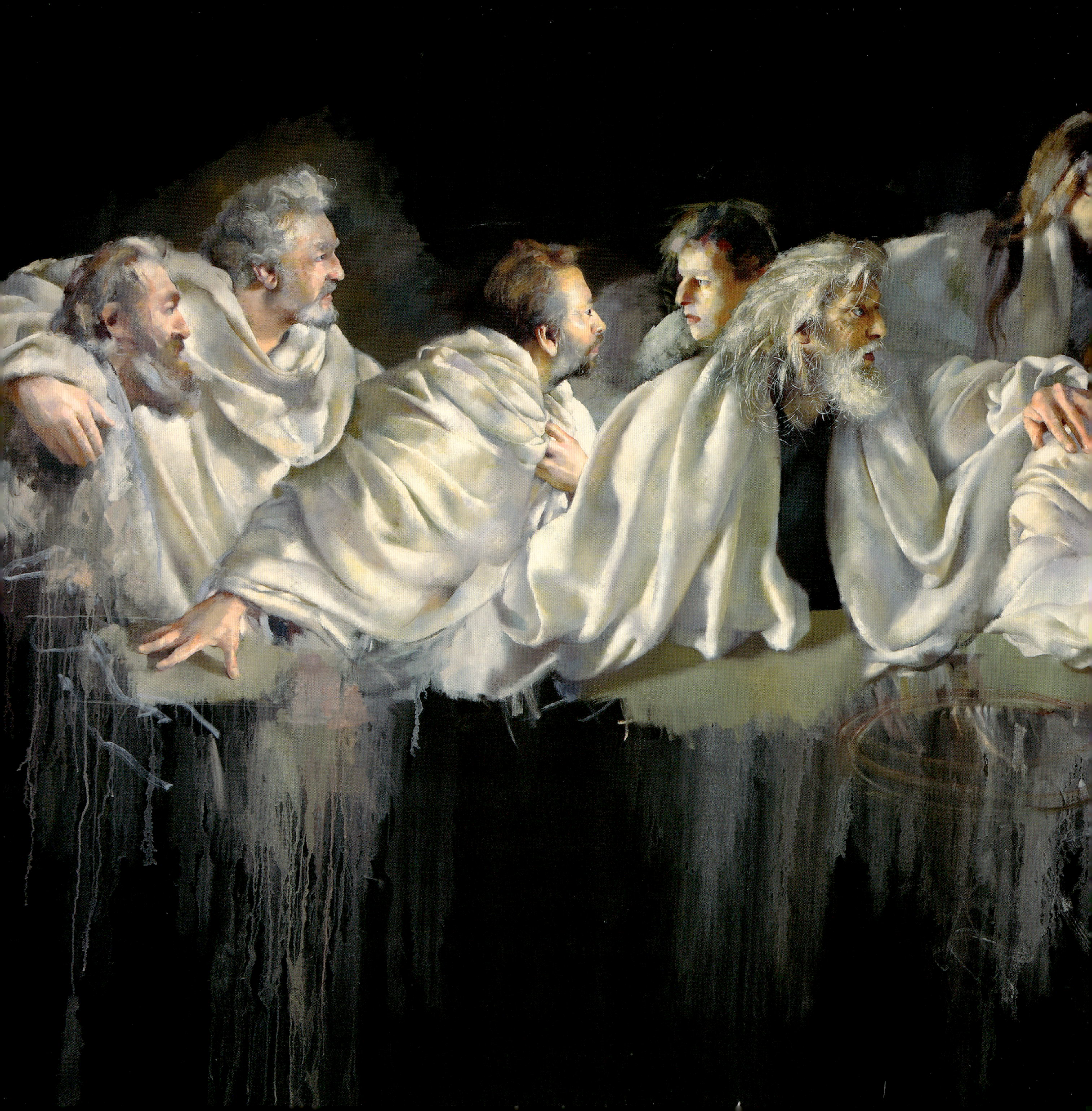

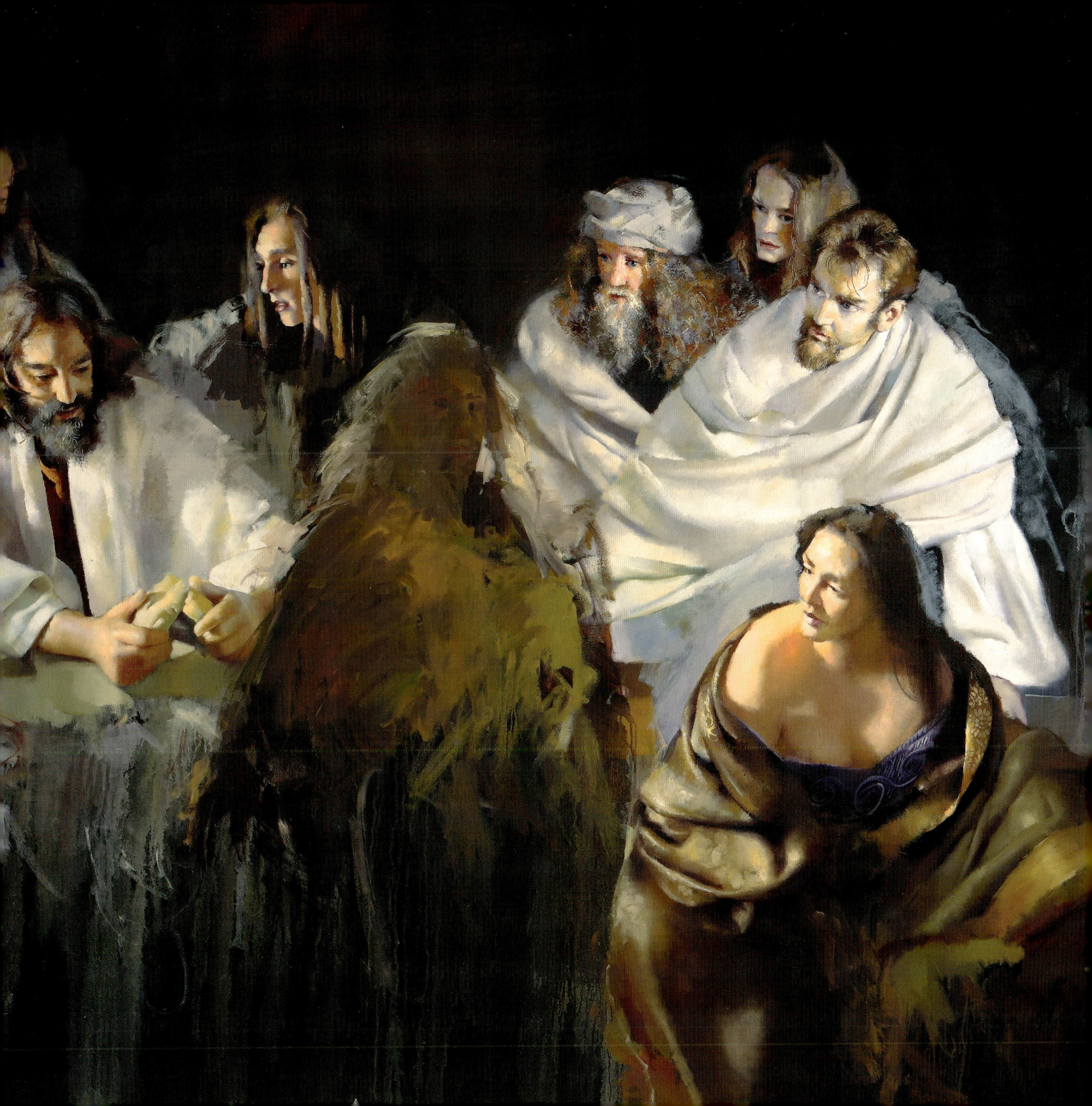

ROBERT O. LENKIEWICZ (1941–2002): CHRONOLOGY

Lars Ramskold

1941 31 December, 8.50 p.m.
Robert Oscar Lenkiewicz and non-identical twin Bernard, born at Middlesex Hospital, London. His mother is Alice Lenkiewicz, born von Schloss-Berg and his father is Ajzyk (anglicized to Isaac) Lenkiewicz. Brother John is born three years later.

1947–1958
Robert attends the following schools: Menorah Primary School, Golders Green; Beckford Primary School, Camden; Harben Secondary Modern, Hampstead; Christopher Wren Technical School, Notting Hill.

1958
At the age of 16, Robert begins at Central St Martin's College of Art & Design.

1959
Robert leaves home at the Hotel Shemtov. He first lives rough in the streets of London, but soon moves in with Ivorene Davis.

1960
After the summer holidays, a 364 ft-long painting of horses at Kilburn stables by Robert was displayed at St Martin's as an example of a hard working student.

Autumn. Robert gets to know Aury Shoa, who has enrolled at St Martin's. They become lifelong friends.

1961
January. Robert meets Celia Mills, who had enrolled at St Martin's in September 1960. A friend says to Robert 'Hey cat, that's one fine mouse you got there'. Robert accordingly nicknames her Mouse, a name she permanently adopts. They become a couple.

June: Robert's first child is born, his and Ivorene's son Dorian.

1962
Robert is admitted to the Royal Academy of Art. Mouse is still at St Martin's as she was two years below him (she leaves quite soon). They live together in London at 4 Eton Avenue.

c.1963
Robert goes on his first trip abroad, to Paris, while Mouse stays in London. He studies paintings at The Louvre.

1964
21 March: Robert and Mouse get married at a registry office in London. Mouse is three months pregnant. They have their wedding breakfast at The Loft, a Hampstead café where they regularly spend much time with friends.

Robert and Mouse move to Gunnislake, Cornwall, for seven months. Robert works as a teacher at St Anne's Primary School.

September: Robert's and Mouse's daughter Alice is born in London.

c.1965
Robert, Mouse and Alice leave London. They rent a house belonging to family friends, Trevawden Cottage, at Lanreath, Cornwall. This is conveniently close to Polmartin, where Mouse's parents live.

1966
13 April: a TV interview with Robert at Trevawden is broadcast.

Early autumn: Robert moves with Mouse and Alice to Plymouth. They stay in various places: Radnor Street; 24 Clifton Street, from where they are evicted; 19 Clifton Street (their friend Terry Goldstone's house, which he shares with them). Robert later buys his own house in Priory Road, the cottage known as Death House, in which Monica Quirk was previously the tenant.

October: Robert's and Mouse's son Wolfe is born.

1967
Monica Quirk moves in with Robert and Mouse at Keppel Terrace, as does the poet James Pascoe. Later that year Mouse moves out permanently.

April: Robert's and Monica's son Reuben is born in Plymouth.

1968
Meets Philip Stokes. Philip will intermittently continue to photograph and document Robert's life. His archive grows to more than 4,000 photographs and five bound volumes of transcribed conversations with Robert.

1969
Robert opens The Portrait Painter studio at No. 25 The Parade (later known as the Barbican Studio) in Plymouth, formerly a vegetable shop owned by Jack Nash. Work starts on *Observations on Local Vagrancy*, afterwards known as the *Vagrancy Project*. Tramps and vagrants fill his home and studios. Robert takes over disused warehouses, nine in all, to house the ever-growing numbers of dossers.

1970

February and March: Robert is tried and convicted for stealing antiquarian books from the Cottonian Collection of The City Museum in Plymouth. Robert claims he sold them to pay for the dossers' food. Robert spends a short time in jail, in Exeter.

1971

Robert meets the Earl of St Germans, Peregrine Eliot. He is soon invited to paint a mural in the Round Room at Port Eliot. The work is never completed.

Robert begins the *Barbican Mural*, which becomes a landmark in Plymouth. It is completed in 1972.

June–July: Robert meets Dutch art student Jeny Lelya Bremer in Plymouth.

1973

March: the VAGRANCY Exhibition opens in Jacob's Ladder at 58 Southside Street, one of Robert's warehouse studios, Plymouth. The exhibition stays open until September.

Robert visits a friend on Gotland, Sweden. He takes the opportunity to make studies for the *Round Room Mural* and the current Project, *Death and the Maiden*.

September: Robert meets Annie Hill-Smith. They will have three children together, but never marry. Robert's daughter Laila is born to Ruti Cohen.

Autumn: Robert visits Amsterdam on Jeny Bremer's invitation, staying at her home in the Jewish Quarter. Robert studies paintings in the Rijksmuseum, and a visit to the Torture Museum gives inspiration for the current *Death and the Maiden Project*.

1974

Mouse and Robert divorce on their wedding anniversary. Mouse has a daughter, Rebecca Lenkiewicz, the playwright, with James Pascoe.

July: The gallery The Fool opens in Plymouth as a collaborative venture between Annie Hill-Smith and Robert to show his Projects.

20 July–1 November: DEATH AND THE MAIDEN Exhibition (Project 2) at The Fool, 7 Clifton Street, Plymouth. This exhibition marks the start of the *Relationship Series: Attitudes Towards Love*, later known as Projects.

10 November–mid-December: DEATH AND THE MAIDEN Exhibition (Project 2) at Wilmas Galleries, Coventry.

1975

20 January–19 March: PAINTINGS DESIGNED TO MAKE MONEY Exhibition (Project 6) at The Fool, Plymouth.

February: Robert's and Annie Hill-Smith's son Sholem is born.

6 May–20 June: PAINTINGS DESIGNED TO MAKE MONEY Exhibition (Project 6) at Blenheim Gallery, London.

Robert visits Amsterdam with Aury Shoa and his son Nahem. In the Rijksmuseum he sees Rembrandt's *The Nightwatch* as it is being restored after damage caused by a knife attack by a mentally disturbed man.

Robert marries Keiko Nakamura, a Japanese artist. The marriage of convenience lasts for 4 and a half years, but they never live together.

16–31 October: LOVE AND ROMANCE Exhibition (Project 4), first at Island House on the Barbican, owned by Royston Lambert, Principal of Dartington College, then at The Fool.

1976

April: Robert's and Annie Hill-Smith's son Jascha is born.

25 August–31 October: MENTAL HANDICAP Exhibition (Project 3) at Jacob's Ladder, Plymouth. Robert's homage to *The Nightwatch* is the centrepiece painting.

1–24 December: LOVE AND MEDIOCRITY Exhibition (Project 5) at The Fool, Plymouth.

1977

25 March: Robert's mother Alice dies. He sketches her corpse at the mortuary – the basis for the painting *Study of the Painter's Dead Mother*.

10 August–30 September: JEALOUSY Exhibition (Project 8) at The Fool, Plymouth.

Robert meets Gillian Pearce, whom he nicknames Mary.

Partial showing of work on the GOSSIP ON THE BARBICAN theme.

1978

23 March: Robert asks Mary 'if she would be agreeable' to being the central figure of a relationship theme exhibition: THE PAINTER WITH MARY. He decides to record his unrequited obsession for Mary in a series of 'aesthetic notes' placed into an elephant folio manuscript.

April: Robert's and Annie Hill-Smith's daughter Kate is born.

10 August–30 September: ORGASM Exhibition (Project 9) at 25, The Parade, Barbican, Plymouth. This is the first Project exhibition in what became the main Barbican Studio.

22 December–5 January 1979: SELF-PORTRAIT Exhibition (Project 10) at the main studio.

1979
26 July–30 September: OLD AGE Exhibition (Project 11) at the main studio.

3 October: Robert travels to Amsterdam, visiting Jeny Bremer. He paints several works for the *Suicide Project*, including Jeny's partner Eddie Agelink (with Samurai sword).

1980
10 August–30 September: GOSSIP ON THE BARBICAN Exhibition (Project 7) at the main studio.

10 August–30 October: SUICIDE Exhibition (Project 12) at the main studio.

8–27 September: RETROSPECTIVE Exhibition, at Blackfriars Gallery (formerly Jacob's Ladder), Plymouth.

1981
4–6 February: Robert fakes his own death as part of the research for the *Death Project*, and to boost sales of *Old Age Project* paintings to benefit Age Concern. The hoax is soon exposed. His brother John, the gerontologist who placed the death notice in a London newspaper, comments 'It seems that the preliminary diagnosis was unnecessarily sombre.'

3–6 February: STILL-LIVES Exhibition (Project 13) at the main studio. Not so much a full Project as a brief pun on the words 'still lives'.

21 March: Robert and Mary get married.

22–28 March: Robert and Mary go to Rome, Italy, on their honeymoon. Robert makes sketches for the Round Room Mural.

16 August–30 September: THE PAINTER WITH MARY Exhibition (Project 14) at the main studio.

1982
Robert meets Karen Ciambriello.

5 October: A TV documentary on Robert, *The Leaves Were Full of Children*, is produced.

6 October–22 December: DEATH Exhibition (Project 15) at the main studio.

1983
30 August–10 November: SEXUAL BEHAVIOUR Exhibition (Project 16) at the main studio. The exhibition is threatened with closure by the police due to concern over an image of the artist (birth sign Capricorn) copulating with a goat, based on a satyr sculpture by Joseph Nollekens in the British Museum.

1984
2 November: Robert's friend and assistant, the vagrant Edwin MacKenzie, 'Diogenes', dies. In accordance with a mutual agreement his body is embalmed, which Robert then keeps as a memento mori in a concealed drawer in the Death Room of the Barbican Studio Library.

1985
8 October: the *Last Judgement Mural* is unveiled in Plymouth's Barbican.

1987
19 July–3 August: OBSERVATIONS ON LOCAL EDUCATION Exhibition (Project 17) at The Great Barn, Chilford Hall, Linton, Cambridge.

Summer: Exhibition at the Crawshaw Gallery, Westbourne Grove, London.

December: Exhibition AESTHETIC NOTES at the New Street Gallery, Plymouth.

1988
1 April–30 October: OBSERVATIONS ON LOCAL EDUCATION Exhibition (Project 17) at the main studio.

19 April–3 May: Exhibition of various works at Polmorla Gallery, Wadebridge, Cornwall.

March: Robert's and Karen Ciambriello's daughter Thaïs is born in the canopied Spanish bed at the main studio.

17 December–28 January 1989: THE PAINTER WITH WOMEN Exhibition (first preview show of Project 18) at the New Street Gallery, Plymouth.

1989
February: Robert's and Megan Clay's son Isaac is born.

28 December: Robert's friend and model Albert Fisher, 'Bishop', dies. Local authorities move quickly to secure the body before Lenkiewicz can act on his written agreement with Fisher that his body should be embalmed.

1990

January 1990: Exhibition THE PAINTER WITH WOMEN: OBSERVATIONS ON THE THEME OF THE DOUBLE (second preview show of Project 18) at the New Street Gallery, Plymouth.

3 September–2 October: Exhibition PAINTER WITH WOMEN: OBSERVATIONS ON THE THEME OF THE DOUBLE. *Folly of Wise Men* studies (third preview show of Project 18) at the New Street Gallery, Plymouth.

1991

April: Robert's and Karen Ciambriello's daughter Chaya is born.

Robert meets Anna Navas.

1992

Robert undergoes treatment for dilated cardiomyopathy at Derriford Hospital, Plymouth.

Halcyon Gallery 10th Anniversary Exhibition (with works from Project 18), at the Halcyon Gallery, Birmingham.

1994

8–15 January: Exhibition THE PAINTER WITH WOMEN (Project 18) at The International Convention Centre, Birmingham.

The Lenkiewicz Foundation is established. It receives charitable status in 1997.

1995

Robert undergoes heart surgery at Harefield Hospital; a quadruple coronary bypass is performed.

13 August–30 October: Exhibition LANDSCAPE (Project 19) at The Barbican Museum and Library Annexe, Plymouth.

1996

29 January–30 April: Exhibition PIECES OF VAGRANCY (a follow-up of Project 1) at The Barbican Museum and Library Annexe, Plymouth.

1997

The book *R.O. Lenkiewicz* (ISBN 0 95 31370 07) is published by White Lane Press, containing extensive interviews with Robert in addition to illustrative material.

9 August–22 October: Exhibition R.O. LENKIEWICZ – RETROSPECTIVE, Plymouth City Museum and Art Gallery, Plymouth. Exhibition opened by Sir Terry Waite.

1998

11 April–6 June: Exhibition R.O. LENKIEWICZ – A RETROSPECTIVE, at Wolverhampton City Art Gallery, Wolverhampton.

2000

Robert receives an honorary doctorate from Plymouth University.

July: Exhibition PAINTINGS PAINTED BLIND – ON THE THEME OF BLIND TOBIT (Project 21) unveiled by the artist for the first time at The Mission, then exhibited at New Street Gallery, and then at The Annexe, Plymouth.

2002

5 August: Robert Lenkiewicz dies from heart failure.

Although the artist's Estate is valued at £3.5m, Lenkiewicz leaves debts in excess of £1.7m. The Executor arranges auctions of paintings from the studio and the sale of the artist's £1m antiquarian book collection.

2003

18 September: 1st studio sale: Sotheby's, London.

20 November: 1st library sale: Sotheby's, London.

2004

15 February: 2nd studio sale: Fenner, Tavistock, at the Theology Building, New Street, Plymouth.

23 October: 3rd studio sale, Bearne's, Exeter.

2005

5 August: publication of the book *A Portrait of Robert Lenkiewicz: Photographs by Dr Philip Stokes* (ISBN 0 95 31370 66) by White Lane Press.

2006

24 June–6 August: Exhibition UNCOMPROMISING STUDY, Hartlepool Art Gallery, Hartlepool (*The Painter with Mary in Newspaper Magi-fools Hats* is exhibited).

October: publication of the book *Robert Lenkiewicz: Paintings & Projects* (ISBN 0 95 31370 90) by White Lane Press.

2007

3 February–26 March: Exhibition TRUE TO LIFE: FREUD, AUERBACH, BOMBERG, LENKIEWICZ AND THE NEW BRITISH REALISTS, at The Herbert, Jordan Well, Coventry.

7–24 February: Exhibition WORKS BY ROBERT LENKIEWICZ at the Halcyon Gallery, Bruton Street, London.

10 May: 2nd library sale, Lyon & Turnbull, Edinburgh.

29 September–18 November: AT THE EDGE: WORKS BY R.O. LENKIEWICZ, 1941-2002. Hartlepool Art Gallery, Hartlepool.

29 November–25 January 2008: AT THE EDGE: WORKS BY R.O. LENKIEWICZ, 1941-2002. Novas Gallery, London.

2008
12 April: 4th studio sale, Bearne's, Exeter.

17 May–30 August: Exhibition ROBERT LENKIEWICZ: LATE WORKS, at Gallery Oldham, Oldham.

26 September–16 November: Exhibition SELF-PORTRAITS: 1956–2002, at Ben Uri Gallery, The London Jewish Museum of Art, London.

Lars Ramskold is a Swedish scientist with a PhD in paleontology, who now works as a dentist. He became interested in the life and work of Robert Lenkiewicz in 2006, and has worked on the timeline ever since.

ACKNOWLEDGMENTS

Lars Ramskold wishes to thank those contributing data to the timeline: Annie Hill-Smith for time and endless patience, Aury Shoa for stimulating discussions, Mouse Mills for lifting the veil from the 1960s, Nahem Shoa for generous assistance, and Chris Raven for invaluable help.

Thanks are also due to (in alphabetical order): Esther Dallaway, Sharon Davidson, John Lenkiewicz, Francis Mallett, Chris Nichols, Mark Penwill, Brian Prowse, Paul and Ben Somerville, and Peregrine St Germans, all of whom have assisted in various ways.

Undoubtedly many errors and omissions remain – they are all the responsibility of Lars Ramskold.

Self-Portrait Aged 15. 1956.
Oil on board, 27 x 17 cm.

Self-Portrait. c.1956.
Oil on paper, 29 x 18 cm.

Self-Portrait With Letter. c.1957.
Oil on canvas, 174 x 100 cm.

Self-Portrait Aged 17. 1958.
Oil on board, 59 x 49 cm.

The Painter With Diogenes. 1973.
Cryla on masonite, 84 x 77 cm.

Mr R. Lenkiewicz. 1973.
Oil on canvas, 80 x 60 cm.

Self-Portrait Aged 32. 1973.
Oil on canvas, 46 x 30 cm.

The Painter With Courbet's Self-Portrait. 1974.
Oil on canvas, 121 x 76 cm.

Self-Portrait With Monica (diptych). 1975.
Oil on panel, 36 x 23 cm. (left panel of diptych).

You Offer Me a Dead Rose, May I Give You a Dead Rat? 1976.
Oil on board, 41 x 56 cm.

Self-Portrait With Mephistopheles. 1978.
Oil on board, 102 x 61 cm.

Self-Portrait. 1977.
Oil on canvas, 51 x 45 cm.

Self-Portrait. 1978.
Cryla on board, 40 x 28 cm.

Self-Portrait. 1979.
Oil on canvas, 75 x 62 cm.

Self-Portrait With Mary with Newspaper in Her Hair. 1980.
Oil on canvas, 127 x 127 cm.

The Painter With Mary in Newspaper Magi-Fools Hats. 1981.
Oil on canvas, 48 x 69 cm.

Self-Portrait Fantasising Playing Mary Like a Cello. 1981.
Oil on sailcloth, 51 x 43 cm.

The Painter Holding Himself When Ninety. 1982.
Emulsion on canvas, 145 x 99 cm.

The Father Eats His Son. 1982.
Cryla on paper laid on board, 84 x 66 cm.

The Painter With Patti Avery. St Antony Theme. 1989.
Oil on canvas, 97 x 86 cm.

Self-Portrait as St Antony Listening. 1993.
Oil on canvas, 122 x 122 cm.

The Painter, Early Morning. No Saturated Colour,
No Saturated Pain. 1995.
Watercolour on paper, 37 x 29 cm.

The Painter With Anna. 1995.
Oil on canvas, 121 x 119 cm.

The Painter in the Wind, 3.50 a.m., July. 1995.
Oil on board, 51 x 43 cm.

Self-Portrait With Hourglass. c.2000.
Oil on canvas, 110 x 61 cm.

Self-Portrait Holding Philippe Aries'
In The Hour of Our Death. 2000.
Oil on canvas, 110 x 61 cm.

Self-Portrait: The Painter in Hospital. 2002.
Oil on canvas, 67 x 72 cm.

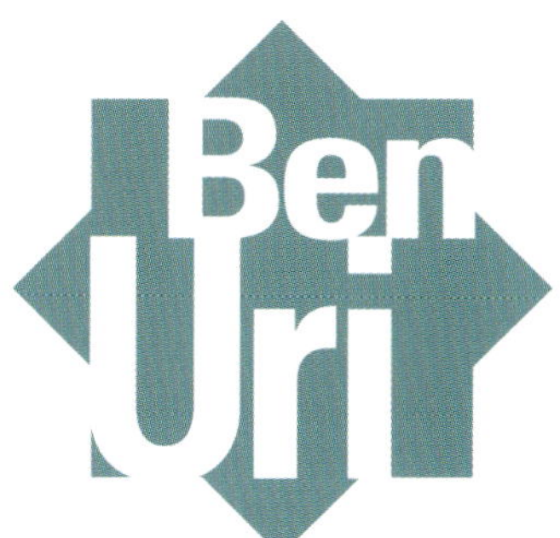

The London Jewish Museum of Art
A Museum for Everyone, Bridging Communities through Art